Understanding Faith

—

An Exploration of Theology

To Cheryl & Lynne —

Blessings & best wishes

to two great publishers.

Keep on running

CW Allfreeman

St Nicholas', 1998

Understanding Faith

—

An Exploration of Theology

C. W. McPherson

MOREHOUSE PUBLISHING

Morehouse Publishing
P.O. Box 1321
Harrisburg, PA 17105

Morehouse Publishing is a division of The Morehouse Group.

Printed in the United States of America

Cover design by Trude Brummer

Note: A study guide for this book is available on the Internet at www.morehousegroup.com.

Library of Congress Cataloging-in-Publication Data
McPherson, C. W.
    Understanding Faith : an exploration of theology / C. W. McPherson.
        p.   cm.
    Includes bibliographical references.
    ISBN 0-8192-1767-0 (pbk.)
    1. Theology, Doctrinal—Popular works.   2. Episcopal Church—Doctrines.   I. Title.
BT77. M39   1998
230'.3—dc21   98-39096
                                                                              CIP

Contents

- 1 -
A Preface to Theology

We shall not cease from exploration
And the end of all our exploring
Will be to arrive where we started
And know the place for the first time.
                                    —T. S. ELIOT

First things first: why a new study of theology? Because the Church is in crisis, and critical periods provoke theology.

That is the most honest answer which can be offered. It also demands an immediate explanation. A crisis, despite the usual connotations of the word, is not necessarily a negative thing, nor a thing to be avoided at all costs: it can on the contrary be something overwhelmingly positive. It must, however, involve profound and comprehensive change, and that is precisely what has happened to the Christian Church in recent memory, and what is happening at this present moment. It is why I, like many practicing Christians, find myself thinking about theology more consciously, more intentionally, and more often.

Crisis comes from a Greek word meaning "judgment" or "decision." Wise counselors know very well that a birth or a marriage is just as much a crisis in the life of a family, community, or individual as is a death: the common factor is radical change, a completely new direction. The change may involve profound joy just as it may involve numbing pain. A "hinge moment" in life may, paradoxically, involve both. In a larger sense, while childbirth and marriage seem "happy" events, and death "sad," all three involve the critical element of disruption of the normal flow of life, and the heightened consciousness that accompanies such disruption.

The Christian Church in our era has been faced, from within and from without, with decisions and judgments, with choices and challenges, which have long since passed the critical stage. From without, the Church has been confronted with a host of ethical questions raised by the existential circumstances of late twentieth-century life, ranging from the consciousness of a single global community to the potential for universal destruction, from the place of Christianity in an increasingly pluralistic theological context to the problems of hunger and population. From within, the Church has been challenged by its increasing sense of ecumenicity, resulting in a longing for a unity lost many centuries ago but scarcely regretted, scarcely missed, until quite recently. The Church has been challenged by the increasingly compelling presence of the Pentecostal and charismatic movements, with their concomitant appreciation of the emotional and individual expression of spirituality, and by various manifestations of reform and reaction within the more traditional Churches.

This entire study has been written, for reasons which will become apparent, from the perspective of the Episcopal Church and its world context, the Anglican communion, but this Church is in many ways emblematic: the challenges it has faced have been faced to a lesser or greater extent by all of the other Churches which used to be called "mainline denominations." These challenges have included the revision of liturgy (of which the current revision of the Book of Common Prayer is the most visible example), the issue of inclusiveness in leadership—the decision to ordain women, for example, has been an outstanding example of this issue having been decided and put into action—and the enormous ethical shift from a symbiotic relationship with the dominant secular culture and a symbiotic reinforcing of its values (an "Erastian" position) to a countercultural, prophetic voice.

These are not the usual and inevitable changes any organization or organism experiences over time; these are deep issues, and they involve paradigmatic shifts, shifts in identity and self-understanding. Any one of these challenges would have been substantial. Their confluence has already marked this era as the most radically critical since the Protestant Reformation of the sixteenth century when a similar list of paradigmatic changes recast the entire Church in the Western world.

Such critical change involves often bewildering complexity and often daunting paradox. Theology is, among other things, an attempt to come to grips with the complexities and paradoxes of the faith. Crisis provokes theological thought and feeling; it is the irritant that produces the pearl. In the earliest Church, the challenge of certain heretics provoked two monuments of Christianity, the New Testament canon or table of contents, and the classic creeds.[1] The fall of the Roman Empire—an unprecedented horror for all concerned, Christian and non-Christian alike—provoked Augustine's mightiest theological statement, *The City of God*. The shattering intellectual revolution of the twelfth century provoked the great Summae of the Middle Ages, including Thomas Aquinas's magisterial *Summa Theologiae*,[2] the single most ambitious theological work ever written. Of course, the transvaluation of values we call the Renaissance provoked the theological work of the Reformation and Counter-Reformation.

Within its far more modest limits, this study attempts to respond to exactly the same sort of provocation—to a paradigmatic shift and a critical moment. Virtually any such moment involves a share of confusion and discomfort. That pain may be what has given the word *crisis* its exclusively negative connotations. But childbirth also involves pain; growth involves pain; love involves pain. As physicians have begun to realize, understanding in and of itself helps to mitigate pain. Understanding sheds light. It also lightens the burden and eases the way.

Thus this new study of theology.

In what sense "new"?

Several senses of the word are noted briefly here and elaborated throughout the rest of the work.

First, the subtitle, a theological "exploration." The implications here are intentional. The field of Christian theology, although it has been exploited for two thousand years, remains I believe an open field, with many untouched areas. Although it has been partially cultivated, and cultivated quite well, it remains partially unexplored. It always will. Theological study in the past has given the impression of closure, of comprehensiveness; ours will be uncharacteristically tentative, deliberately nondeliberate, open-ended. It will have more the open and "unfinished" quality

1. Please see chap. 6.
2. Sometimes also referred to as *Summa Theologica*, a less accurate title.

of much twentieth-century art than the finish and closure of, say, the Baroque.

As a corollary, the study will be a personal exploration; hence, I use the first-person word "I," and the second-person "you." This is not meant to suggest an informal or colloquial quality, but is central to my intention. I am not so much offering a "new" theology, or advancing "my" theology, as inviting you into the process of theological thought and imagination. This is meant to be—to use a very contemporary catchword that suits our purposes exactly—an interactive theology.

Second, the philosophical approach. Virtually all theology uses philosophy as a tool, or, as the medieval thinkers called it, a "maidservant," an *ancilla*.[3] Philosophy allows a controlled, conscious approach to the subject, rather than a random one. This is especially important if our overall model is exploration. My philosophical toolbox is provided by the analytic school of philosophy. This is new, in that no other general study of theology has exploited it—not as a creative tool. It has been used to criticize, but never to synthesize. Why it has not will, I think, become apparent as we investigate this school of philosophy.

Third, our study of theology will be, within its limits, holistic. Issues of liturgy, worship, scriptural scholarship, history, and spirituality will be introduced which, in the past, have often been considered to be beyond the purview of "systematic theology" (or, before that, of "dogmatic theology"). The word holistic has become unfortunately popular in theological and other intellectual circles—it sounds a bit trendy—but it happens to be the precise word here. We are working on an understanding of theology which involves the whole of faith experience, not the rational or traditional doctrines of God, though these will be admitted, explored, and assessed. As the great twentieth-century philosopher of religion Rudolf Otto asserted in his basic work, *The Idea of the Holy*, our theological experience is only rational in part, and

---

3. Of course, this was both sexually and economically a biased metaphor. But a metaphor it was. Theologians did not tend to be able to afford maid- or manservants.

perhaps not the "deepest" part. A comprehensive approach to theology will acknowledge the other aspects of human experience and perception that participate in our experience of what Otto called the *numinous*, the ineffable and the uncanny.

This is part of the reason the whole is written from *within* the Anglican Communion, rather than from a supposed Christian vantage point outside any particular Church. We will be referring throughout to liturgical practice, to the Book of Common Prayer, to historical events, to ethical developments, and so on, which make the best sense in the concrete, actual, incarnate experience of a practicing Church.[4] The ancient principle of *lex orandi, lex credendi*, "the law of worship is the law of believing," which finds many of our most deeply held theological principles not in doctrinal statements but in the words of weekly and daily worship, will be employed throughout.

The word *whole* is etymologically related to the words *healthy* and *holy*. In Old English, the earliest stage of this language of which we have record, they were the same word. The same idea obtains in the patristic[5] concept of the "analogy of faith," that theology was not one compartment among many, but rather a unifying principle for all aspects of faith. Any thinking Christian could be called a "theologian"—not just those who did rarefied academic work. The earliest theologians all seem to have been busy with either diaconal, episcopal, or monastic duties to the extent that it is a marvel they produced any writings at all.

In this sense, our approach will also be synthetic—it will aim at a synthesis, an overarching vision—although it will begin with analysis. The Belgian Catholic theologian Desire Joseph Mercier, commenting on the relationship of philosophy to science, wrote that, while the sciences always remain analytic, "sound philoso-

4. Any interested reader from another context should easily be able to translate and transpose these things in such a way as to make them useful to him or her; none of this material is arcane or obscure.

5. The period of Church history from the age of the apostles until roughly the sixth century. A key era in the formation of the Church at all levels. See chap. 6.

6. Report quoted in de Wulf, *Introduction to Scholastic Philosophy*, pp. 263ff.

phy sets out from analysis and terminates in synthesis."[6] I take this precept to be all the more applicable to theology. After a time of analytic challenge and trial in both disciplines, a new synthesis seems highly desirable, however daunting such a project must seem initially.

Fourth, our study will freely interact with the secular realm, with secular culture. It is intended to be culturally, as well as theologically, holistic. It is my deep conviction that twentieth-century art and science in general support, rather than undermine, Christian theology, contrary to the impressions of most and the convictions of many. To act on this conviction, I must freely allude to or quote many secular ideas, for example, which are not normally thought of in a theological context, and I must refer to developments in fields such as quantum mechanics or modern astronomy, in which many have felt a negative challenge to the faith.

Another way of stating this concern might be that it is a task of theology to investigate the relationship between Christian faith and the contemporary world. The investigation should not encompass contemporary values, nor fashions in thought, but the honest, rational, partly empirical picture culture always provides of what is real. This is particularly important because, in the past, Christianity seemed so congruent with a prevailing worldview. The multistoried, hierarchical, rational, geocentric universe of the later Middle Ages, for example, has often been portrayed as entirely consistent with Christianity.[7] The question now is whether Christianity and the worldview bequeathed us by the twentieth century—which is complex, not hierarchical; paradoxical not rational; and in which no center can "hold"—is also consistent with genuine Christianity, as opposed to the cultural Christianity Reinhold Niebuhr criticized.[8] My contention obviously is that the twentieth century proved to be surprisingly supportive of Christianity, but understanding that contention involves a great deal of explanation.

---

7. For example, by F. Lovejoy in *The Great Chain of Being*, E. M. W. Tillyard in *The Elizabethan World Picture*, and C. S. Lewis in *The Discarded Image*. A less-known but insightful work by C. N. Cochrane, *Christianity and Classical Culture*, does the same for the earlier era.

8. In *Christ and Culture*.

What then does the word *theology* mean for this study?

The word is composed of two rather transparent Greek root words, *theos* and *logos*, which can be translated simply "God" and "word." *Theology* therefore can mean "the word about God," or a discussion of God. "Do you believe in God?" is an opening for theological discourse.

This simple definition, as an educated guess at the word's denotation or strict meaning, works rather well. Unfortunately, *theology* has all sorts of connotations, many of them negative. Since connotations form part of what a word means to those who use it, we have to take these connotations seriously. No word "is" its denotation only; every word "means" more.

For many unchurched people, for unbelievers, and for people with marginal and nominal church affiliations, the word *theology* can connote something quite remote from everyday reality. It can connote something precious, quaint, and dated, like a Victorian postcard, which is pleasant in a harmless way but not to be taken very seriously. *Theology* can represent, in short, the extreme example of the ivory-tower mentality. Even educated persons associate theology with the rarefied, irrelevant disputes in which the medieval Christian thinkers were supposed to have indulged, such as speculations about the number of angels dancing on the head of a pin. This speculation itself is, essentially, a modern legend about medieval thought rather than a problem on which the medieval philosophers ever wasted energy.

For many within the Church, the word *theology* connotes something entirely different but similarly negative. For this group, the word has come to stand for a cold and rigidly intellectual process, a rationalizing of a belief they treasure as living reality. For persons "seeking ordination," as it is rather awkwardly and a-theologically put, the word can mean nothing short of a necessary evil, a temporary part of a hazing process to be endured with little or no actual benefit—a concept to be relegated to the short-term memory then disposed of as one begins "real ministry."

Both sets of connotations, like all impressions, relate to real experience. Theology can certainly be precious as it can be rigidly intellectualized. But these connotations are also extremely unfair to the subject itself. Genuine theology is, in the first place, far more than a jejune version of Sunday School, and far more than an academic exercise. Theology at its best and at its center represents an attempt to express the emotional, intellectual, psychological, and physical impact of a living Being. It is powerful, not precious. It is for serious people, not frivolous fantasists. If it is sometimes difficult to understand, that is because the realities with which it deals are sometimes complex and difficult. Theology can tax the limits of human reason and imagination along with theoretical physics, which, for the same reason, similarly strains the limits of human thought. Theology can also tax the emotions; it can exhilarate and devastate. Tragic literature and great music can also perform this function and again for analogous reasons. They probe and provoke the limits of human feeling. This is part of the reason the contemporary Roman Catholic theologian Hans Urs von Balthasar has intentionally constructed a system that admits the aesthetic media as a means of theological expression (as does the Protestant Hans-Georg Gadamer). Great art, like theoretical physics, can actually express realities inexpressible by any other means. As we shall see, our own system will assume this principle and offer examples of poetry, not as decorative embellishment, but to express the substance of our encounter with God.

This point bears further examination, since throughout this exploration we will be referring to both art and science as major correlatives of our theological understanding. For all its complexity and no matter how compelling intellectually, science, which throughout the twentieth century has acted like a voracious black hole in relationship with philosophy, always *simplifies* reality. That after all is the essential meaning of "abstract thought." Aspects of reality have been "taken away" in order to reveal more an interesting principle. Science offers models of reality for this reason: a model is always simpler than the reality it represents, whereas an equally complex representation is called a "replica." Art, by contrast, deals with ambiguity, paradox, and open-endedness, and, for our purposes, above all with complexity. A physical equation that "suggests" more than it contains would be considered a weak equation. A poem that "suggests" more than its literal meaning is considered normative. In his seminal study, *Mimesis*, literary critic Eric Auerbach claimed that the two fundamental types of Western literature were defined by Homer and by the Torah. Homer is all surface detail, clear and complex, but unambiguous and rational. Torah is all depth, with very little surface detail (where is Abraham ever *described?*), but like a bottomless well in its suggestive quality. Analogously, we might say that science aspires to the Homeric style, art to the biblical. Like Auerbach, we assert that the two do not contradict but rather complement one another.

Negative connotations of the word *theology* have falsely limited its meaning. The two root words have themselves been limited. A work of popular theology two decades ago illustrated limits placed on the word *theos* in its title, *Your God Is Too Small.* This accusation has an even greater application than its author imagined. Many people, whatever their religious identity, seem to conceive of God in startlingly narrow terms. Apparently most have never outgrown images and explanations of God provided when they were very young, and therefore think of God in the most simplistic ways, and of theology as an absurdly juvenile pursuit. The God explored by centuries of serious theology is, by contrast, multifaceted, complex, challenging, and, as we shall see again and again, often characterized by paradox—at least from our perspective, which may conceal the yet more important simplicity.

The greater problem remains with the word *logos.* It is, as we have noted, commonly translated "word," but like the Hebrew *torah*, which is translated "law" but includes far more, *logos* covers more meanings in Greek than "word" in English. First, *logos* is also the root of the word "logic," including therefore the ideas of reasoned, sequential thought, problem solving, and planning. For example, assume that you dislike everything you have read so far and have decided to return this book for a refund. How will you do that? What steps will you take? What sequence of events are you imagining right now? Everything from the human problems you anticipate with the salesperson or manager at the store, to the route you will take to get there, to the checkbook adjustments you will need to make—all that constitutes a logos.

But even that is not nearly enough. Bertrand Russell, who represents an endpoint in the divorce between philosophy and theology, but whose linguistic analyses we will nevertheless find helpful, understood logic in this linear, sequential sense only, and declared further that there can be no true knowledge which cannot be approached through this narrow logic. He was followed by the early Ludwig Wittgenstein, who determined that metaphysics itself—the "content" of traditional philosophy—was impossible, because it rested on assumptions that could not be verified in a logical way. The same attitude, usually unexamined, lies behind the disdain many scientifically minded persons have held toward theology.

The ancient meaning of the word *logos* provides the key which springs this mental trap. Logos meant, as we shall see when we examine its theological use,[9] any principle of expressing the ineffable. A reasoned argument has its logos, but then so does a well-written poem, a work of architecture, a symphony, a painting, an appealing arrangement of flowers, or a problem in physics.

Theology in the early Church retained something of this broader sense of the root word *logos*. Theology was "done" through reasoned, articulate discourse, but it was also done through liturgical hymns and psalm singing, by poetry, by the painting of sacred icons, by the shaping of sacred space. The logos of theology involved the imagination as well as reason. It pointed to any expression of the sacred and ineffable reality of God. Preeminently, then, it applied to the writers of the Gospels, which are works of imaginative art as much as works of discursive reasoning.

Theology, understood in this broader sense, should be more compelling. It should hold intrinsic interest for any serious Christian person, whether layperson or ordained leader. Within the Anglican communion, theology should appeal to layperson, bishop, deacon, or priest. Our communion is often characterized as "nonconfessional," meaning members need not adhere to a catechetical confession. This is quite true, meaning that it is all the more, not less, important for serious members to understand their theological options. The Episcopal Church in the United States represents one of the broadest spectrums of belief and style in all of Christianity and may be the most "inclusive" of all

---

9. See chap. 5, "A Christology," below.

communions, incorporating extreme sacramental conservatives along with extreme evangelicals and charismatics. A strong grounding in theology can center the serious believer in what could be bewildering religious chaos.

Even more important, Christianity is preeminently a faith of the Word. *Logos*, as we have seen, is broader than "word," but that is its central meaning. Therefore, *theology* is central for the faith. That faith is communicated in words more than any other means. It has been concerned from the beginning with hard, rational reflection on religious experience, treasuring a set of books as Holy Scripture. Our denomination, moreover, has always employed a Book of Common Prayer for regular worship.

Our faith is thus indisputably verbal. We believe and we worship "in" words, however important the nonverbal, phatic experiences also involved. The concept, moreover, of God's self-communication through the Word—a concept we will return to and examine several times—is normative for Christian faith. We believe that in the work, words, and, above all, the person of Christ, God articulates God's self, or, as St. Ignatius of Antioch puts it more imaginatively, we believe that Jesus is the "mouth" of God.

For whom is this study of theology intended?

It is intended for any person interested in thinking seriously about Christian faith and tradition. It is not therefore directed specifically at the theological specialist, whether student or professional. At the same time, this is not a work of Christian apologetics, the normal genre for the wider audience, but rather aspires to be a contemporary systematic approach to what used to be called dogmatic theology. The study thus intends to meet several different needs. In general, a serious, systematic approach to theology should, as I have said, employ new philosophical tools and insights and demonstrate awareness of contemporary trends and developments in other arts and sciences, but should at the same time demonstrate awareness of and sensitivity to the traditional categories of theology—creation, sin and redemption, atonement, resurrection, pneumatology (doctrine of the Holy Spirit), ecclesiology (doctrine of the Church), eschatology, and Christology. These are technical terms, but they stand for living and vital realities. They are anything but irrelevant, academic abstractions. We will explore each of these traditional Christian realities, albeit from the somewhat new angle permitted by the philosophical tools we shall borrow.

Further, I believe in what educators call "spiral learning," and not just theoretically. With a subject as complex as ours, spiral learning seems the best way to do justice to it. Therefore, returning to the same ground—but from a different point of view— would seem the best way to approach theology. I have tried to write the material so that it is accessible to various levels of learning and sophistication. My hope is that the utter novice and the advanced student will be satisfied, along with everyone in between. I hope to accommodate both the complete beginner, who has had neither a church school background nor training in philosophy, and the student who has already studied systematics, probably in seminary or college, and therefore is already conversant with the themes of theology and some of the traditional approaches.

My work is produced in a fallen world, however, and therefore both students may be frustrated from time to time—the beginner by things he or she does not quite understand, the experienced theological student by things too elementary. Of both, I simply ask patience. The spiral always manages to catch up with the reader, or vice versa.

One corollary, on a slightly different subject. I have mentioned that I deliberately include extensive allusions to other fields of learning and culture. I do this because of a serious conviction that theology is relevant to the rest of the world and should be in constant conversation with science, philosophy, current history, and the arts. My approach is in fact the very opposite of that of some religious conservatives who oppose conversation between theology and science. I believe twentieth-century science has supported, rather than undermined, Christian theology, and theology in general. To make that assertion, I have to know something about quantum theory and the principle of indeterminacy, for example, and thus I have to mention such things. However, such material is almost always illustrative only. I try never to establish the "main points" with reference to such material. Therefore, if any of this ancillary material seems unfamiliar do not be concerned that it will keep you from following the train of thought. That train is actually on a straightforward track.

Finally, just as we have broadened the sense of the word theology, we should broaden the sense of the word *theologian*. The ancient Church understood any serious practicing Christian to be a theologian. It is not merely a discipline or profession or a special vocation within the Church. The task is incumbent upon all members, who, by virtue of their baptismal vows,[10] proclaim by word and example the good news of God in Christ. No one can deliver a message he or she does not understand, and no one can bear a message without a means to express it.

Anyone serious about the faith, any adult intentional about discipleship, is, then, already a theologian. Presumably, the reader of this sentence is a theologian. If your image of a theologian is of a remote and abstracted academic, or of a rarefied and ghostly religious, please revise it, or rather broaden it. A theologian is one who takes God seriously, who tries to understand his or her own faith and to communicate it as part of Christian identity and vocation. The purpose of theological study—of this study—is to deepen and clarify that identity and to help you enjoy that vocation more profoundly—to make you better at it. In the words of a joyful paradox of St. Augustine, theology aims to help you become what you are. As I asserted at the beginning of this section, I am less interested in advancing my theology than in serving as a catalyst for yours.

---

10. We will examine the recovery of the colossal importance of baptism later in the text. Baptism expressed among other things our *common* Christian identity, that which all Christians, regardless of Order, shared.

-2-
An Analytical Approach

Wovon man nicht sprechen kann,
daruber soll man schweigen.
— LUDWIG WITTGENSTEIN

Whereof one cannot speak,
thereof one should be silent.
—LUDWIG WITTGENSTEIN

It is the responsibility of systematic theology to explore the traditional categories, for these are its subject matter. It is also the responsibility of systematic theology to explore those categories in new ways. These are our two criteria for serious theological inquiry, and the two complementary principles by which I mean to guide our work. Theology is a discipline, among other things, and no discipline is static: it develops, it grows. In this it probably resembles the arts more than sciences. The sciences do apparently progress as problems are solved and information is acquired. The arts cannot legitimately be said to progress, but they do change form and develop, like living organisms. It is then the responsibility of theology to stay current. We cannot believe in a *theologia perennis,* however much we believe in perennial truth.

The expression of theology has always depended on philosophy. In the Middle Ages, philosophy was therefore considered the "handmaid" of theology, a servant that gave theology ways of expressing theories and truths, models and paradigms. Philosophy, it must be understood, is not primarily a study of idea systems, but rather an approach to problems. The use of philosophy in theological work, for example, does not assume adherence to any particular philosopher's worldview.

Thus, in modern times, serious Christian theologians have borrowed the philosophical categories of Karl Marx, a materialist and an atheist who would have dismissed their theological work as nonsense. In the middle of the patristic period, a number of Christian theologians made extensive use of the philosophy of

Plato—particularly of his reality model or ontology—who would themselves have rejected his views of God and his proposals for an ideal state. Medieval theologians such as Thomas Aquinas and Albertus Magnus used the theology of Aristotle, newly revived in the West, to tremendous effect, elucidating sacramental realities Aristotle himself would probably have found utterly bewildering. The sixteenth-century reformers borrowed freely from the secularist, humanistic philosophizing of the day.

Theology in the twentieth century has been no exception, with serious use having been made of several leading philosophical trends. For decades, the popular text for systematic theology in our denomination has been John Macquarrie's *Principles of Christian Theology*, an exceptionally good work that fulfills our two criteria perfectly. Macquarrie treats the traditional themes of theology at length and sheds new light in almost every instance by using the approach of the modern philosophical school of phenomenology, especially as developed in the thought of the German philosopher Martin Heidegger.

My own approach derives instead from the Austrian Ludwig Wittgenstein, who developed certain tendencies of British philosophers into an analytical philosophy. In a limited and digestible way, what I am trying to develop is an *analytical theology*, concerned at every point to analyze the words we use to express theological theory and experience. This seems appropriate, given a religion based on the Word and expressed primarily in words. The guiding questions often will be, What exactly does this word mean, or, what does it point to? How is it functioning? Does it "work" for us? Where our answer seems to lead us to believe that words have "failed" us, that we are trying to express the ineffable, we will fall back on the aphorism of Wittgenstein quoted at the beginning of this chapter: whereof we cannot speak, thereof we should be silent.

At this point, a reader acquainted with modern philosophy may hesitate, realizing that the philosophical "school"[1] to which we

---

1. The quotation marks merely suggest that "school" is used loosely. Like most philosophical schools of thought, the analytical is really a tendency and a trend.

have just alluded has been understood as incongruent with Christianity. The names Wittgenstein and Bertrand Russell suggest hostility to the faith, especially Russell, who was proudly and self-consciously "anti-Christian," though what he opposed most now would recognize as a fossilized institutional Christianity. How can one introduce such a philosophical approach into a faithful Christian theology?

This is the reason we tried carefully to define philosophy as an approach to thought, as a tool, a means to an end. Existentialism has often been similarly understood as antithetical to Christianity, probably because Albert Camus and Jean-Paul Sartre, its most famous exponents, albeit not its most central philosophers, were adamantly anti-Christian. But existentialism has been recovered as a powerful possibility for Christian expression. It is not only that important precursors of existentialism like Blaise Pascal and Søren Kierkegaard were deeply theological thinkers. More important, Christian theologians such as Paul Tillich and Macquarrie have made significant theological use of existentialist method.

My approach is to use the method of analytical philosophy to theological ends. This has in the last three decades been tentatively attempted. As I understand the Anglican tradition, it supplies a more ready and comprehensive vehicle for expressing the content of theology and can serve to make traditional Christianity more accessible, more relevant, more credible to a world which has suffered through the twentieth century.

To use a thought-system that at first seems inimical to the faith is nothing new. The classic examples mentioned earlier of theologians who used philosophy were in every case examples of such use. When Thomas Aquinas tried his experiment with Aristotle, the established Church resisted. Aristotle was pagan, therefore anti-Christian; he had not been accepted, as Plato had, by long-standing tradition, and was not *anima naturaliter christiana*, a soul by nature Christian—though he was soon to enjoy that status. For all we can conjecture, the early translation of Christianity into Hellenistic terms, which we see in the New Testament, was resisted by the Jerusalem Church. How would the apostle James have felt about the opening words of the Fourth Gospel—if indeed he ever read them, or had them read to him?

Augustine wrestled with this matter and gave the classic Christian answer in his book *De doctrina christiana*. Should Christians make use of non-Christian intellectual tools? Yes, Augustine concluded. A weapon is a weapon, so let us ransack the devil's armory, or, as he put it, "spoil the Egyptians." His colorful language is what I mean to express more prosaically when I speak of "tools." Augustine took over the toolbox of the deeply pagan Cicero, which supported his eloquence enormously. If analytical philosophy can open similar insights into theology, we can make use of its modern tool kit.

Language and Paradox: Do you see what I see?

Do you see what I see?

This question helps introduce ordinary language philosophy, part of the philosophy of analysis. It is the sort of question Wittgenstein and Russell often ask. It also occurs to thoughtful children, but most adults learn to regard such questions as trivial and impractical. Rare are those adults who continue to ask such questions and to explore their implications. Wittgenstein did, to great effect, as did Einstein, whose insights in the realm of physics often began with such "thought-problems," rather than with abstract equations. We shall likewise resort from time to time to such startlingly childlike, deceptively profound questions, striving for the open mind of a child—a prerequisite, after all, for the Kingdom of Heaven.

Wittgenstein was concerned with both the limits and the potential of language. He saw the great paradox of language, parallel to the human paradox expressed in Psalm 8. Language is, on the one hand, the most effective means of communication human beings have; on the other hand, it can virtually define our limits of perception. A simple thought-experiment may serve to illustrate this point. Imagine that a dog with an ulcer; a four-year-old child, with the same ulcer; and a reasonably intelligent adult with the same ailment. The dog will groan and thrash on the ground. Its master will know little more than "something is wrong." The child will say "my stomach hurts," or less, but the parent will know a good deal more than the dog's owner, because the three words have communicated volumes of information and eliminated even more false possibilities. The adult will say, "I have a burning sensation in my upper left abdomen. It comes and goes, but I feel it most when I am hungry, and it becomes unbearable when I am upset. Do you think I may have an ulcer?" The series of words—and the patient may be able to add hundreds more, as any physician knows—has communicated all sorts of information. Sign language or pictures might have communicated more than the child could, but not nearly this much.

Reflection on this reality might tempt us to think of language as a virtually limitless tool. It begins to feel very God-like, in fact, to be able to do what we can with words. We almost begin to feel the creative power God displays in the first chapter of Genesis, where by word God brings the cosmos into being. Only we as humans, not other creatures, have words at our disposal. One can intuit that words are powerful, magical, uncanny, and also that they are uniquely ours—ours and God's. You and I have just been sharing, probably unconsciously, in their miraculous quality. My one-sided supply of words has enabled us to cover a great deal of ground already. When you answer and question, how much more communication will be possible.

The limits of language, however, can be demonstrated by trying to describe chocolate. Those who have tried realized long ago that it cannot be done, but those who have not tried may find this surprising. Chocolate seems ordinary, a thing we know from childhood. Yet words fail us utterly when trying to describe it. No matter how eloquent you may be, you cannot describe the taste of chocolate; you cannot come close. Words can communicate where chocolate comes from, how it is made, its history, its use in cooking, and its peculiar combination of hydrogen and carbon atoms. But you cannot describe its taste. Why?

There is nothing wrong with your command of the language, nor is there anything wrong with the language itself. Certain experiences, however, must be prior to language for language to work. For example, one can taste chocolate before ever speaking the word. The science of optics recognizes certain primary colors. Similarly, a number of primary words, which cannot be defined, serve as labels for realities like the taste of chocolate, which we know by experience but which we cannot define. Colors fall in this category as well. Describe "red" and you will either draw a blank, or, more likely, try using adjectives such as "hot" or "energetic," which do not describe any color but relate to emotional associations. The eighteenth-century philosopher John Locke called such words without definitions primary ideas, or "simple ideas," because of his concern to determine which mental activities are innate as opposed to acquired. For our purposes, the word *red*, since it is inexplicable, is primary.[2]

It is true that modern physics allows us to quantify things like the color red in terms of wavelength and frequency. We can also assign numbers to sound to locate loud sounds on a continuum. This process, however, is not the same as description. Description must convey sensation to another person, and numbers do this for "red" even less effectively than words such as "hot" and "energetic."

Wittgenstein extended this principle to large concepts and asked, How can we describe God when we are unable to describe the smell of coffee? We cannot. We cannot convey to another sentient being our experience of the reality of God. That is why mysticism resorts quickly to the indirect language of poetry, and why there is so much poetry in Scripture.

Do you see what I see? You and I stand on a ridge, overlooking a sunset together. I see a blood-red orb, about the size of a nickel held in my outstretched hand, becoming gradually redder, disappearing into the horizon. Do you see what I see? Are you sure? Little children (and eighteenth-century philosophers) wonder: does "red" look the same to you as it does to me? What if you see blue when I see red, because that is the way your eye works? Nothing in science can prove your red is not my blue, just as no quantification can convey what colors are. Until some-

---

2. Locke believed that all knowledge, like that of the color red, is acquired knowledge. We have only the innate propensity for understanding and appreciating, but no a priori knowledge of, anything at all. This empiricist position is not necessary to assign a primary nature to certain terms. Even if the color red were an idea with which humans were born, it would remain primary in the sense of being inexplicable in terms of anything else, or anything simpler.

one transplants a brain successfully into another head, we still will not know.

Part of the fascination of poetry (and poetic prose) is its ability to explore boundaries, to take the private and subjective and put it into words. John Keats somehow can convey, using the subtle resources of poetry, what "melancholy" feels like, its strange mixture of pain and pleasure, loss and fullness, beauty and fear. There is nothing profound or abstruse about what he describes. Most people have felt it at some time or other, as surely as Keats did. But that he can *describe* melancholy—probably convey the meaning to someone who has not felt it—seems almost miraculous, as if he could, in words, convey "red" or "coffee" or "chocolate." Or "God."

The student of theology should be aware of these qualities of words because he or she deals with words often, and because theology often slips into the area of the ineffable or the primary. We all intuitively know what primary words mean, but we end up tying our minds in knots when trying to define them. An analytical approach becomes very helpful when theological discussion quickly and naturally begins to talk about the Sonship of Christ, the Holy Spirit, sin, consubstantiality, divinity, redemption, incarnation. Any bright child can memorize a catechism replete with these words, but no wise adult would claim to understand them. Analysis may help us approach these concepts respectfully and tactfully—yet boldly.

Three Modes of Discourse

One objection to theology we already have touched upon is the well-meant question, "What good is all the rational intellectualizing, academic jargon, and big words when we are supposed to be dealing with the powerful, yet simple, reality of God and God's ways to humanity?" We answered that question with our conviction that theology must at times deal with complex realities.

Theology is not necessarily or always academic, complex, or sophisticated, nor does it necessarily use big words. Effective church-school materials for five-year-olds can present strong theology without big words. Further, much excellent apologetic theology has been directed at mature, intelligent adults, while eschewing the academic or technical. Yet it remains solid theology.

But a great deal of theology is intellectually challenging, couched in academic language, and involves "big" (or at least unfamiliar) words. It is not easy. Such theology feels more like working a difficult math problem than singing a favorite hymn. Why? Because it supplies a human need not supplied in any other way and completes the expression of theology begun by Creed and Scripture.

Here is where our analytical approach begins. Throughout this study we will distinguish among three very different types of discourse. This act of comparison will be fundamental to our theological method. Our experience of what Rudolf Otto called the *numinous* has been expressed, historically, in three forms: the *mythic*, the *symbolic*, and the *catechetical*. Usually, but not necessarily, they appear in this chronological sequence, but the important thing is not their sequence but their "interplay," as the modern Anglican Austin Farrer notes in his *Glass of Vision*. They are distinguishable forms, although they can be blended. Though all three are valuable, each elucidates a certain aspect of the same truth or truths. Theological systems tend to run into trouble when they exalt one of the three forms over the other—Romantics, for example, despised anything but the mythological—or ask one mode to do the work of the other, as fundamentalists ask myth to do the work of discursive catechesis, history, or science.

Let us consider as an example how the three different modes account for the fact of creation. The opening chapter of the Book of Genesis presents a powerful *mythic* treatment of creation—a cosmological story of origins:

> In the beginning God created heaven and earth. Now the earth was a formless void, there was darkness over the deep, with a divine wind sweeping over the waters.
>
> God said, "Let there be light," and there was light. God saw that light was good, and God divided light from darkness. God called light "day," and darkness he called "night." Evening came and morning came: the first day.

God said, "Let there be a vault through the middle of the waters to divide the waters in two." And so it was. God made the vault, and it divided the waters under the vault from the waters above the vault. God called the vault "heaven." Evening and morning came: the second day.

God said, "Let the waters under heaven come together into a single mass, and let dry land appear." And so it was. God called the dry land "earth" and the mass of waters "seas," and God saw that it was good.

God said, "Let the earth produce vegetation: seed-bearing plants, and fruit trees on earth, bearing fruit with their seed inside, each corresponding to its own species." And so it was. The earth produced vegetation: the various kinds of seed-bearing plants and the fruit trees with seed inside, each corresponding to its own species. God saw that it was good. Evening came and morning came: the third day. (Genesis 1:1–13, New Jerusalem Bible)

Serious biblical scholars have realized for many years that this account is related to earlier Mesopotamian creation stories, such as the Babylonian *Enuma Elish*. It is by no means unique as a creation myth. Theologians of the Old Testament such as Gerhard von Rad have further investigated the peculiar theological twist the Genesis version gives creation and demonstrated the ways in which the story, theologically, is unique. In any case, it fulfills our criterion as a myth, in that it expresses truths beyond the reach of discursive prose and ordinary logic.

The Creed expresses the same truth, but in a different way:

We believe in one God,
the Father, the Almighty,
maker of heaven and earth,
of all that is, seen and unseen.

This terse yet still powerful statement results from the symbolic language of the Creed and of certain kinds of theological poetry. The poet Ezra Pound defined *poetry* as "language charged with meaning to the highest possible degree," and, though his definition fails to account for everything most would call poetry, it suits exactly what I am calling the symbolic mode of the Creed, for the latter truly is written in poetic language. In fact, the word for "creed" in Greek, the language in which the Nicene Creed was written, is *symbol*. The word *creed* itself comes from the Latin for the first words in the Apostles' Creed, "I believe." The Creed began out of a need for a concise and exact statement of the essential Christian belief system to be expressed in question-and-answer form at baptism, and developed as a safeguard against distortion of these beliefs. The Creed is therefore terse, but far from a reductive shorthand. The Creed opens more questions than it answers, so condensed is its language: Father? Almighty? Maker? Seen and unseen? All these seem to cohere with a logic beyond logic, but also to cry out for explication.

> This means that the universe is good, that it is the work of a single loving God who creates, directs, and sustains it.

This selection, from the Catechism, displays the explication that the *catechetical* mode tries to provide. The word *catechism* means simply "instruction" or "teaching," and the catechetical mode is in fact common and familiar. Every sermon that attempts to "unpack" theology or Scripture at its points of density, every discussion group or lecture that attempts to express what a passage means, and every casual coffee-hour conversation that turns on theology takes place in the catechetical mode. This study is written primarily in the catechetical mode.

Like the symbolic and mythological modes, the catechetical mode attempts to express truth or truths. Unlike the other two, it attempts to express truth with straightforward, unequivocal language, linear logic, and prose. It cannot express truth completely, but neither can the other two modes. The transcendent reality to be expressed is by definition impossible to explain in any language. In different ways, all three modes point to that reality and complement one another, since they point from different angles.

Throughout our exploration of theology, we will move between the three ways of speaking about God: mythic, symbolic, and catechetical. Our three primary texts will be Scripture, Creed (both Nicene and Apostles'), and catechism. Necessary tools will include, in addition to this book, a Bible—with Apocrypha—a Book of Common Prayer (containing the Creeds at several points), the Catechism, and several historical documents. As a supplement, the reader may consult the bibliography, which lists both modern and classic Christian approaches to theology that have proven helpful through more than twenty centuries of theological work.

Our sequence will follow the Creed, as expanded in the Catechism. Scripture, unlike the Creed, appears in mixed sequence. Almost no sensible reading is accomplished by reading it from beginning to end. Unfortunately, the first and last books of the Bible, dealing as they seem to do with beginnings and endings, can tempt people into doing exactly that. We will begin with the very first word in the Creed, and continue, word by word where appropriate, otherwise phrase by phrase. This approach has a long and venerable tradition. It is essentially Macquarrie's method, and is the method of more popular introductions to theology used in the Episcopal Church, such as Marianne Micks's *Introduction to Theology* and Pike and Pittenger's *Faith of the Church*, contained in the earlier Seabury Series for adult education. The approach more or less follows Norris in *Understanding the Faith of the Church*. It is somewhat artificial, in the sense that it reproduces almost nobody's personal sequence of faith—who really begins a statement of belief with God the Father Almighty?—but has the compensatory virtue of collective wisdom, which, I trust, will become evident as we explore.

-3-
A Christian Anthropology

Know then thyself, presume not God to scan;
The proper study of mankind is man.

—ALEXANDER POPE, *ESSAY ON MAN*

A Point of Departure

The Catechism begins with a heading, "Human Nature," and a question, "What are we by nature?" This may seem strange. Why not begin, as many philosophers begin, and as some theologies have begun, with God, or with God the Father? The subject of theology, after all, is God, and normally we would look elsewhere for a study of "human nature," perhaps to anthropology, history, or psychology. Is this some novel "humanism" or a secularization of the ancient Christian tradition? We have said that our theology will be based on the Catechism and the Creed—does the Creed not begin with God?

In fact, it does not. The first word of the Creed is *we*,[1] and the first section of the Catechism therefore explores that single word. "God" is actually the object, not the subject, of the first clause in the Nicene Creed and the Apostles' Creed. "We" is the subject. Understanding the Creed begins by understanding this word, and understanding this word begins with the question, "Who, and what, are we?" The Catechism and our study follow this logic and attempt to answer that question.

Obviously, one straightforward answer to the question, "who are we?" would be, "those who believe what follows." This is the chronologically primary answer, in that the Creed was written as an answer to problems of Christian belief, definition, and inclusion. The councils of Nicea and Constantinople, which produced the ecumenical Creed, tried to define exactly what Christians did believe—as opposed to pagan thinkers, Jews, Manichaeans, and the permutations of Christianity which had developed during the

---

1. The "we" appears in English translation. In the original Greek and Latin the verb alone expresses the "we."

first three centuries of Christian experience.[2] Christians—
"we"—are the ones who believe in one God as opposed to a pantheon; who believe that God is triune, as opposed to monolithic;
who believe that Jesus Christ is truly God, as opposed to an
inspired prophet; who believe that Jesus Christ is truly human, as
opposed to a phantasm in human disguise—and so on. We will
explore these various antitheses later. Important at this point is
that the Creed sets those holding these views apart from all other
schools of thought and modes of belief. These beliefs are in a
very real sense who "we" are.

This assertion has proven remarkably accurate. The "we" of
the Creed truly represents Christians, and excludes all others.
Outside of the New Testament, there is virtually nothing—no
theological writing, letter, hymn, or prayer—as universally
accepted by Christians in all their bewildering variety. The
Creed has retained that character for sixteen centuries, again,
unlike anything outside the Bible. Orthodox or reformed, Eastern or Western, ancient or modern, Protestant or Roman Catholic,
the vast majority of Christians have found that the Nicene Creed
does what it intended: to provide a consistent, concise statement
of their faith. Even Christians who give the early Church no special authority, who downplay more ancient practices such as the
Eucharist or the sacramental orders of ministry, find that the
Creed serves their theological purposes very well. It is, moreover,
the theological cornerstone of the "Chicago-Lambeth Quadrilat-
eral," the classic modern attempt at Christian ecumenicity.

No one who is not a Christian would assent to much of it, of
course. A great proportion of humanity would accept none of it,
and a still larger proportion would agree only with the very first
phrases—or with the first clause—and reject the rest. As we shall
see, the longest section of the Creed deals with Jesus Christ,
simultaneously setting Christians apart and challenging our
belief. The Creed contains more to offend the non-Christian

---

2. These other permutations were technically heresies but, as will be
noted in the chapter on the Holy Spirit, the word *heresies* has misleading
connotations.

believer than the Lord's Prayer. To the nonbeliever it must represent baffling nonsense. All this amounts to a quintessentially Christian document.

The Catechism, however, goes on to explore other implications of the word *we*. It also refers to humans beings in general—the only beings we know who use words to communicate. This is the largest sense in which any of us uses the word: to mean "we human creatures," as in, "We walk upright on two legs." Therefore, "What are we?" can also mean, "What does it involve to be human?"

That is where our faith begins—not with the experience of God. Like Aristotle, who "begins" philosophy with what we (there "we" are again) already know, and the theologian Thomas Aquinas, who followed him, we begin with human nature. We can paraphrase Alexander Pope: our proper starting point, though not the whole of our proper study, is humankind.

The word *nature*, related to nativity and natal, is not accidental or casual. It means "what one is born with," what one is intended to be, what one originally is. Christianity has so often mentioned our fallen nature that our basic or original nature has been forgotten or emphasized only minimally. Our emphasis on original sin has made us forget that sin is anything but original. Our origin, Christianity maintains, in myth and in doctrine, is sinless. The myth of Eden shows that we were made for paradise, not damnation. The word *fallen* also implies an earlier existence. We cannot be fallen unless at some point we were higher than we now stand. To any who are saturated with certain expressions of Christianity, discussion of our nature is going to sound surprisingly positive, optimistic, and hopeful.

Given that nature describes what we are, not what we have become, what, then, are we? The first assertion is, "We are part of God's creation, made in the image of God." With this statement we are already making implicit assertions about God. These assertions must be clarified later, when we consider God directly, but it is significant that from the beginning we are defining humankind in terms of relationship. The Creed may be approached usefully as a series of claims about relationships between humankind and God, among Father, Son, and Spirit, between Church and Spirit, and so on. In everyday speech, we often define ourselves in terms of relationship: "I am John's mother" or "I am Mary's daughter," rather than "I am president of the bank" or "I am a street sweeper." We are related to God, we assert here in a defining gesture, as creature to Creator.

Simultaneously, we must also note that we are claiming a relationship with everything else. We are part of creation. Thus we claim that we are not alone in the cosmos, that other beings, other creatures, exist. This is no small claim. Descartes, considered the founder of modern philosophy, challenged this claim three centuries ago. How, he asked, do we know "beyond doubt" that anything else really exists? We assume other things exist, but we also once assumed that heavenly bodies circle the earth, for example, and that heavy objects fall faster than light objects. Our senses, Descartes reminded himself, are notorious in their capacity for deception. How then do we know that we are not alone? More accurately, how do you know that you are not alone? This question led in part to the origin of his philosophical system. Descartes devastated the commonsense answer, then carefully constructed a way out of the dilemma.

His achievement stands behind our making the claim. Since we are doing theology, and not philosophy, we will not retrace his steps, but assert the conclusion as part of our faith: we believe in the existence of other creatures, as we believe in the one responsible for creation. The two were hinged in Descartes, who discovered that the only way he could believe in creation was first to satisfy himself that there was a Creator.[3] Sensory evidence has nothing to do with the existence of either one.

What does it mean to be created in the image of God?

"Made in God's image" is what distinguishes us from everything else that exists, from the rest of creation—made, but not in God's image—and from God's self, existent, but not made. This is what the logic of language tells us. Being "in God's image" separates humanity from the genus "everything that is made." The

---

3. The next chapter will investigate Descartes's approach to the existence of God.

second question follows naturally: what does it mean to be the Creator's image?

The visual origins of the word *image* must be immediately corrected. It does not mean that we think of God in human terms.[4] *Anthropomorphism* is the word anthropologists use to describe religious cultures which create gods in human image. The classical gods, for example, are anthropomorphic, shaped more or less like ideal humans.[5] While admiring the sculptor's art, we tend to assume that we have advanced theologically beyond any crude belief in manlike gods. But our problem may be more subtle. We may attribute human urges for power, domination, causation, and control to God, thinking that these attributes belong to God because we are supposed to be made in God's image. Thus we may be tempted by an insidious, since it is unconscious, anthropomorphism just as misleading as a mesomorphic statue of Zeus.

The assertion here, rather, is that to be made in God's image means that "we are free to make choices: to love, to create, to reason, and to live in harmony with creation and with God." This is the attribute we share with God, and these are the verbs we have in common. We can also assert attributes of God—omniscience, omnipotence, omnipresence—that we do not share. We do not know everything, we cannot do everything, and we cannot be everywhere. We do share love, creativity, reason, and the potential for harmonious existence with God. Curiously, our capacities in these four areas are not limited.

That we are free to make choices is the first attribute that God shares with us, the first gift or *charism*. It is a staggering claim, but because the capacity it names seems so familiar, its magnitude is usually lost. We take the ability to make choices for granted. The idea that God shares attributes with creatures is ancient. Psalm 19 begins, "The heavens declare the glory of God, / and the firmament shows his handiwork" (Book of Common Prayer), and theologians throughout the ages have expanded and interpreted this

---

4. Compare the discussion of apophatic theology in the chapters below.
5. Whether any thoughtful Athenian in the fourth century B.C. believed in these gods is debatable. In the first century B.C., Cicero and his circle found them silly (see the *Tusculan Disputations*).

statement to mean that God shares God's vastness with the sky, depth with the ocean, beauty with the stars, and so on. But the word *image* requires something far more essential to God's being than these attributes. The ability to make choices fulfills that requirement. This is both a tremendous theological claim and a commonsense observation. It is common sense because, as far as our experience informs us, it is literally and pragmatically true that we alone among creatures in our ability to make decisions, to affect the outcome of events, to make plans, and to think about the future. One does not know exactly when one will finish this book. On the other hand, it is your choice whether to slam the book shut or continue reading. No other animal—cat, dog, or fish—can make the choice. We take the ability for granted, precisely because the ability has been granted, as surely as starlings have been granted the gift of flight and cats the gift of jumping nimbly and powerfully.

In traditional theology, this commonplace reality lies behind the vexed question of free will. If we are able to choose, we must be free. If we are free, we can make choices. There is no such thing as an unfree choice. If an option is predetermined, it is not an option.[6] In claiming that we are free to choose, we set ourselves against the philosophical stance of determinism, according to which our actions—along with everything else—are predetermined by a divine being or abstract principle such as "necessity." Karl Marx's philosophy of dialectical materialism is a version of determinism, invented by altering the premises, but retaining the basic shape, of the doctrines of G. W. F. Hegel, the nineteenth-century metaphysician. Determinism represents a classic approach to reality, well known in the ancient world. It was in part to fight this doctrine that Augustine formulated a substantial portion of his teaching, especially *De libero arbitro*, "On Free Will." Augustine explains that unless there is free will, Christianity is illogical. Christianity is concerned with the reality of guilt, and no creature

---

6. This idea becomes subtle in the philosophy of Kant, who saw that the power to possess or to do anything is not freedom. If our desires are predetermined or conditioned, then we are not free, but are slaves to these desires.

can be guilty if its actions are determined. Thus, we never refer to an animal as guilty, except in jest or in metaphorical discourse. We believe that beasts are compelled only by instinct, conditioning, and reflex, and that they do not make choices. In a Christian anthropology, will must be paramount, prior even to rationality and knowledge. As twelfth-century Scholastic theologian Peter Abailard maintained, contrary to customary belief, we can incur guilt as long as our will is operative—even when we do not know and understand. Why else, he asks, does Christ pray from the cross, "Forgive them, for they know not what they do"?

The infinitive "to love" stands first among the choices for a reason. If we are God's image, it follows that our basic nature would reflect God's. And God, as we shall assert below, "is" love. When we examine this assertion in detail, we will examine the ramifications and history of the word *love*. For now, we can define the word provisionally as "an act of the will, sometimes supported by feeling, which directs us toward the happiness and well-being of another person." It is the opposite of instinctual selfishness. The problem with the word is that we use it most often to express two emotional states, themselves mutually distinct. The first use of the word denotes simple affection, as in "I love examining the etymological implications of ordinary words." The second use describes comprehensive sexual attraction, as in "Abailard loves Heloise." Neither of these uses is what we mean when saying one is free to love, which involves action and not feeling.

Perhaps more strongly than any other theologian, Peter Abailard, besides providing us with a parenthetical example of erotic love in the previous paragraph, emphasized Christian love in his system of thought. Beginning with the premise that God is love, he continued by saying that Christ reveals this love—both of which we assert in the Catechism. But Abailard is virtually unique in his claim that what Christ does for Christians above all is to provide an example of incarnate love for them to follow. Our assertion in this catechetical anthropology parallels Abailard's assertion. We are free to love because we are God's image.

J. R. R. Tolkien, the Christian novelist and scholar of medievalism, forbade use of the word *creative* in his classrooms, as in "that poet is very creative." Tolkien reminded his students that, strictly speaking, God alone is creative, since only God creates ex nihilo, "out of nothing." The best humans can do is to imagine and imitate.[7] The same can be said of any attribute. It is true of love as well, for, as God's images, all humans can manage is a mere reflection of the love that moves the cosmos. Yet if we remember that God has endowed us with the capacity to choose, we see that these attributes must be real. God has shared free will with us. We can act freely and, therefore, we can assert that God has shared a measure of divine creativity. We are creative beings—not just metaphorically, but in substance.

It is a fact that all humans create. I am not using the word in the narrow sense of accomplished artistic creation, though many individuals and cultures have intuited that there is something divine, or at least supernatural, about such giftedness. The Greeks spoke often of creative artists, the sculptor and poet, as possessed by a *daimon*, a numinous, extrapersonal presence, and meant practically the same thing as contemporary references to "God-given talent."[8] But I am trying to replicate the sense of the word as found in the Catechism, the sense in which anthropology speaks of *homo faber*, "the human as toolmaker." Naturalists have recently discovered that chimpanzees (who are, as biologists in their turn have informed us, our closest relatives in that their genetic code is 98% identical to ours) use sticks as extensions of their fingers to retrieve termites and other grubs. But other than these chimpanzees, human beings are the only creatures known to create in the limited sense of rearranging materials for new purposes. We are the only creatures who make anything for aesthetic reasons. Every known culture produces works of decoration, such as adornment for the body, and even small children seem naturally to produce artwork.

---

7. Tolkien was a true product of the Western Christian tradition and thoroughly familiar, as a medievalist, with Augustine and his successors in the West, who stressed this doctrine. Eastern Christian thought has been more open to the idea that God shares attributes, and therefore more hospitable to the idea of human creativity. What follows in this analysis is more in harmony with the Eastern tradition.

8. In some Greek tales, Apollo, Hermes, or the rebel Dionysus appears as the giver of artistic creation.

In a more fundamental sense, creativity relates to the capacity for decision making, for choice, which we have already examined. Reason is also important here, which to our post-Romantic ears can sound forbidding and cold. But reason and creativity are closely allied.[9] Whenever a schedule is made or a plan devised, creativity and reason conspire—they "breathe together"—to produce something that otherwise would not exist. We tend to overlook humbler, everyday examples of human creativity, the things we do "all the time." But the difference between them and Rembrandt is logically just one of degree, not of kind.

Even these ordinary acts are God-given or, better, they are God-shared. They are important moments in which God shares a facet of the divine nature. Genesis expresses the concept mythically. Before the Fall, God invites the human creature to share in the last stage of creation, the naming of the other creatures. Up to this point, God has done all the talking, which has all been creative and has involved bringing creatures into being by word. The freshly made human is invited to take over the poetic work of creation.

As we have just suggested, reason has been disparaged ever since the Romantic revolution in aesthetics and the thought of the eighteenth and early nineteenth centuries. It is still popularly distrusted. People are urged in many contexts to "express what they really feel," or to "get their emotions out." Reason is condemned through the use of derogatory epithets ("head trips," "hair splitting," and hundreds of others). Various reasons for this anti-intellectualism have been adduced, but most agree that the Romantic movement made a significant contribution. Leading Romantic artists such as Keats, Shelley, Wordsworth, Blake, Goethe, and Schiller were said to condemn reason as cold and inhuman, and to have freed the soul by the expression of emotion

---

9. The Romantic notion of artistic creation as antirational is a fiction. Romantic artists were as deliberate and rational as any of their predecessors. The most famous example of "irrational" creativity is the report that Samuel Taylor Coleridge composed poems in a trance. This was a biographical deception. Prophets may compose in a trance, but no poet, to my knowledge, has ever done so.

and feeling. I use the words "said to" deliberately, for their approach was far more complicated. What has been made of their thought they themselves would scarcely recognize.

At any rate, by using the word *reason* in the Catechism we intend something rather broader than its popular definition, just as the catechetical sense of *creative* is broader. We do not mean narrow step-by-step reasoning involved in solving a problem in algebra. The catechetical use of the word includes that sense, but far more of the mental landscape as well. By *reason* we refer to something like what the Greeks called *nous*, the capacity to think, in sequence, and of our own volition. This meaning incorporates far more than the ability to follow a Euclidian scheme, or to put two and two together. One of the pre-Socratic thinkers, Anaximander, considered this trait so important that he projected it onto the cosmos, called *nous* "God," and gave reason the prominence that Western Christian tradition would later give love.

But such extrapolations are unnecessary to understand the centrality of reason to our experience. Its importance can be demonstrated by an everyday occurrence such as losing your keys. Without "thinking" about it, you "think out" a plan, retrace your steps, and ask yourself, "Where did I have them last?" Gradually the search expands, if necessary, to other people via media such as the telephone. The process, if fully documented, would turn out to be far more complex and systematic than it "feels," but that is only because we are so adept that we take the steps for granted. Even in such a mundane context, we exercise the power or talent or gift of reason—just as surely as Einstein used his gift when he worked out the theory of special relativity.

When humans think through problems, they are doing something that is apparently unique to the species. No other creature of which we are aware thinks *through* anything—with the probable exception of the chimpanzee with the stick. In his later work, Plato, while avoiding for the most part the extreme position of Anaximander, believed that thought was the highest function of humankind, the divine spark. Some of his followers gave reason divine status. We Christians, more moderately, assert that reason, like love and creativity, is an attribute God shares with us.[10]

This phrase from the Catechism again describes a relationship between humankind and God, between humankind and the rest of creation. The phrase affirms that we are not created out of synchrony with either God or our fellow creatures. To use a twentieth-century word, the alienation we feel is chronologically, or at least logically, secondary, though quite real. We are not created with a propensity toward evil, but with a capacity for it—a distinction that has too often been lost. When, in the words of the old confession, we admitted that "there is no health in us," we did not mean that we were created sick. *Health* meant "means of healing," not a state of freedom from illness in the current sense. The fourth-century priest Pelagius denied this interpretation, claiming in essence that we are able to heal ourselves. We are not, as we shall soon assert.[11] We were free (to speak mythically) never to have become sick in the first place; however, God did not condemn us by our nature to be imperfect beings.

This freedom further suggests that we are not, by weakness or finitude, inherently incapable of living in harmony with God and creation. It is not blundering or weakness which causes our alienation. In an era of increasing ecological awareness and global consciousness such reasoning may sound familiar, though the word *harmony* suggests an ancient reference. The word conjures the idea that God made the cosmos on a musical model, as a thing of beauty in which each part contributes its portion of the tune. The Pythagoreans articulated this idea in the fifth century B.C. with enormous seriousness, and Christians revived it ages later. The

---

10. Tracing the historical development of this Christian notion is beyond the scope of this work. That reason should be exalted is not a New Testament idea. A similar approach would be the *Logos* theology of the Fourth Gospel (see "A Christology," below). Reason becomes important when the apostolic writers wrestle with their classical context and achieves an apogee in Aquinas, *Summa Theologiae*, pt. II.

11. Pelagius has had many disciples. The perspective of the twentieth century makes him seem almost ridiculous, but at the end of the nineteenth century a modern Pelagianism swept the Western world.

idea is apparent in the system of Dante in the fourteenth century, and it lies, mythically, behind this catechetical section.

With regard to harmony, our investigation of Christian theology can remind us of the often neglected fact that Christianity is Oriental in origin, not Western, and that it is kin to other Oriental systems. In a strict sense there have been no major Western religions, only antireligions such as rationalism and materialism and nationalism. That Christianity, more than any other faith, has been espoused by Westerners does not make it Western. A good case could be made that attempts to acclimate Christianity to Western experience and values have distorted and even falsified it. At any rate, in common with the other great faiths of the East, Christianity assumes as an ideal an orderly, harmonious cosmos, in which humanity "plays its part" but does not conduct the work. Everything is connected, as John Donne asserts in his homily "For Whom the Bell Tolls," and as the Buddhist proverb states: "The beating of a butterfly's wings on the Pacific affects the mountains in Tibet." Taoism and Shinto, indigenous religions of China and Japan, both stress harmony with nature as the "chief duty" of humankind. Confucianism and Hinduism likewise stress the importance of nature.

Christianity is kin to these theologies of the East. What is strange to Christian thought is the modern Western assertion of the individual, Nietzsche's "will to power," the ideal of competitiveness, the survival of the fittest, and the dichotomy of body and mind. Political notions such as the white man's burden (chiefly British) and manifest destiny (American) are corollaries of these more fundamental philosophical tenets. Though these notions seem almost quaint today, it is healthy to remember that just a generation or so ago they were considered with the utmost seriousness, held to be part of the Christian scheme, and preached from Christian pulpits.

To live in harmony with God is the Christian ideal, and this does not mean to excel or dominate. That much may be easy to accept. But the statement also refers to not fulfilling or asserting the self, which may be more problematic. Christianity runs counter to a psychological culture of self-fulfillment.

The Catechism next asks, "Why then do we live apart from God and out of harmony with creation?" and suggests a response: "From the beginning, human beings have misused their freedom and made wrong choices."

Here is another clear-cut example of the Catechism expressing in other words a reality stated in two other sources. The question and response are first expressed mythically in the second chapter of Genesis and throughout the book.[12] Symbolically, the Creed acknowledges one baptism for the remission of sin. Later, the Catechism will examine the concept and reality of sin in detail, but here the word is intentionally avoided. Why it was avoided I hope to make clear.

First note that the Catechism reverses the order of the Genesis story. In Genesis, as in all myths of a fall from paradise, the story follows the sequence of (1) original happy state, (2) sin, and (3) punishment. Genesis represents the stages with (1) life in paradise; (2) disobedience of taking forbidden fruit; and (3) expulsion from paradise, resulting in the current condition of the human race. The Catechism, by contrast, begins with the fact of alienation and explains the state as having resulted from wrong choices. In later sections of the Catechism we will encounter the alienation as sin, but here we receive our first catechetical answer to the question why life is the way it is.

At first glance, this explanation sounds weaker than "because we are sinful" or "because we sin." It sounds almost innocuous. Should we suffer because we make wrong choices? We want to point out that wrong choices are not our fault. We say, "I'm not guilty. I just made a mistake." Sin implies knowledge. We say that a person sins only if he "knows what he is doing." The Genesis mythology reinforces this concept, because the humans in the story know what they are doing.

Our tradition stands in opposition to the classical concept in this matter, as exemplified by the teaching of Socrates. Wrongdoing always results from wrong choices, Socrates taught. Wrong choices result from ignorance. Thus, evil enters the world not because of willful intent, not because of guilt or sin,

12. See, for example, Gerhard Von Rad's *Commentary on Genesis.*

but because of ignorance. If we knew better, we would always do what is right. Judeo-Christian tradition denies this belief categorically, asserting instead that evil will precedes all corrupt thinking. Nor is ignorance ever an excuse. As Peter Abailard pointed out in his *Ethics*, "making a mistake" does not guarantee guiltlessness; otherwise, what sense was there in Jesus saying from the cross, "Father, forgive them, for they know not what they do?" (Luke 23:34).

Further, Christian tradition teaches that the results of sin are pervasive, including death and destruction, but also everyday angst, the common cold, and mistakes. All are evidence of our fallen state. The problem with beginning with *sin* is that that word is already theologically loaded. For too many people it connotes a spectacular, peculiar, and by definition rarely encountered event: murder, theft, adultery, libel and slander, blasphemy, and the like. These actions are sins. But so is the minor-key "sin of omission," the fleeting wave of disdain, the cruel comment, the half-witted double entendre, the careless disposal of garbage.

These also are sins, but many find it more natural to call them wrong choices. Whatever the terminology, these events transpire every day and affect each of us. Had the Catechism started with sin, we might have overlooked them as unimportant.

The degree of willful intent is a classic problem in the field of ethics and has perplexed philosophers from Plato to Immanuel Kant. Based on the conviction that any ethical act must be conscious and "universalized," Kant formulated a "categorical imperative," a philosophical version of the "golden rule" stating that actions should be desirable for the one and the many. Important for our theological understanding is that wrong choices imply consciousness. "Wrong choices" do not refer to honest mistakes, but choosing the bad deliberately over the good, with the knowledge that second best is equivalent to the bad.

An experiment in ethics involves asking yourself what you would change if you could relive the past six hours. The odds are that you have not murdered, stolen, or blasphemed. You are probably no great sinner. Nevertheless, if you understand the experiment, and unless you are unusually centered spiritually, you will find around six things to change.

Your wrong choices did not all result from innocent ignorance. Most were probably the result of those weaknesses we label "irritability," "fatigue," "bad mood," "preoccupation," and so on. We recognize the "wrong" involved, but it does not seem significant enough to call "sin."

But as Jesus makes clear in his teachings on anger and adultery in Matthew 5, wrong is merely a matter of degree.

Now in no sense does this discussion lead to the conclusion that we should become scrupulously conscious of these wrongs. That is the way to neurosis, not health. The catechism approaches sin as "wrong choices" primarily because sin is a larger category than most people imagine with more of our behavior contained within than we know.

Why do we make these wrong choices? Let us begin with the myth of Eden. Schoolchildren who first hear the story of Adam and Eve often think, "I would do better. They had it made. Why give it up just for some rotten fruit?" We are told that the fruit was very appealing—not rotten—but anyone can see it could not be worth life without pain, friendship with God, and peace among creatures. That same rational child within us says that we would be shrewd, that we would not throw paradise away for the sake of forbidden fruit.

But of course we would. *Adam* is not a proper name in Hebrew, but a common noun meaning "man," as *Eve* means "woman." This myth is about humanity, not a prehistoric forebear or an eponymous ancestor. Though some poets have, interestingly, tried to imagine the attractiveness of the fruit itself,[13] that is not the point of the story. The point is that the fruit is forbidden, and therefore any object would have sufficed as a lure.

The explanation for the prohibition—that it will endow the creatures with divine knowledge of good and evil—is really just an aspect of limitation. Humanity rebels against limitation. We want absolute freedom. Our freedom is not absolute, however, and in the first of many paradoxes we shall encounter, the pursuit

---

13. See, for example, John Milton's *Paradise Regained*, in which the temptation scene carefully depicts the fruit as appealing to each of the Seven Deadly Sins. But this is eisegesis, imposing meanings on the text.

of absolute freedom serves only to restrict us terribly. As Augustine said, in God's service is our perfect freedom.

The traditional theological category for human rebellion is *pride*. This word is, if anything, more problematic than *sin* since it stands in part for a reality that is not sinful. We speak of pride in one's work or family, and these forms of pride are in no sense sinful.

What is meant by pride, theologically, is what the Romans called *superbia*. It describes, in terms of the spatial metaphor of altitude, a sense of superiority. The Catechism explains the word as putting oneself in the place of God. In terms of the Eden myth, one refuses to acknowledge a prohibition and chooses a forbidden food said to make one godlike. This choice shows that human beings want to be in God's place.

The choice of forbidden food can also be understood as a crime against an orderly creation. God having made us, according to Genesis, the pinnacle of created order, but second to God's self, desiring the first position is wrong as well as foolish. A vivid parallel occurs in the Greek story of Phaeton, human son of Helios the sun god. Offered any wish, Phaeton insists on taking the sun god's place as driver of the solar chariot, and ends up as a falling star.

That dynamic of falling is important. The first section of the Catechism, like Genesis, its mythic parallel, and Psalm 8, its poetic analogue, depicts a sudden, swift, and precipitous fall from the most exalted creaturely status to the most debased. The dynamic from this point is upward and Godward as we begin to turn from the creature to the Creator.

Q. What help is there for us?

A. *Our help is in God.*

When a new bishop is ordained, he or she pronounces a blessing reserved for bishops, which begins, "Our help is in the name of the Lord." The response, spoken by all present, is "the maker of heaven and earth." By our principle of *lex orandi, lex credendi* ("the law of worship is the law of believing"), this is not merely a happy custom. It is a theological assertion, initiated by the newly ordained person as a symbol of unity in the faith. It is basic to our understanding of ourselves and of God.

Our help is in God. This is also a defining point in the Catechism. To define means to set limits, to establish boundaries, to
point to *differentiae,* and this is the difference between us, between
the "we" of the first phrase of the Creed and all other systems. It
is not a pious sentiment, but is central to who "we" are.

Other systems of thought recognize everything that we have
thus far asserted about humanity, that we are alienated and that
"things are not as they should be." The difference lies in where
the impetus comes from for changing these conditions. The difference lies in the answer to that question, "What help is there
for us?" Our answer sets us in the strongest, starkest contrast to
the philosophy of humanism.

The idea of secular humanism has recently become a bête
noire in popular Christian discussion, as if it were a diabolical
innovation. Secular humanism is a serious and respectable modern school of thought. Humanism, strictly speaking, is any philosophy or anthropology that understands human beings as having
the innate means or potential for their own improvement. Such a
philosophy states that humans at least theoretically can improve
their lot, unassisted by any outside force or agent, whether God
or fortune or karma. The term itself, *humanism,* dates to the Western
Renaissance of the sixteenth and seventeenth centuries. At that
time, the scientific work of Galileo and Johannes Kepler and the
philosophical work of René Descartes—none of whom were
themselves humanists—enforced the intellectually popular
notion of the supreme potentiality and power of human reason.[14]

The humanist attitude itself, however, is far more ancient. As
has already been suggested, this doctrine took a quasi-Christian
shape in the teaching of the fourth-century priest Pelagius. The

---

14. Descartes's philosophical work may have been the most powerful
contributing factor. Descartes attempted, or at least saw the possibility of, a
unified theory, mathematically based and mathematically deduced, that
would account for the entirety of physical reality—something Einstein in
his latter years worked hard to achieve. Descartes's philosophical work ran
parallel. He determined to establish a metaphysics rooted entirely in
absolute rational certainty. To the popular mind, these efforts looked a great
deal like prying open all the mysteries of heaven and earth, but Descartes
himself was far too intelligent to think that way.

attitude is implicit in the teachings of Socrates as far as we can reconstruct them, insofar as he believed that reason leads inevitably to goodness and that right thinking leads to right action. It is even more implicit in the teachings of the philosophers he attacked, the Sophists. They believed humanity to be the "measure of all things," as one of their greatest representatives, Protagoras, is supposed to have said.[15]

Humanism came into vogue in the eighteenth century, in the Age of Enlightenment, and the epigram for this chapter from Alexander Pope represents a partial expression of it in an era that witnessed a pervasive belief in the supreme power of human reason. It enjoyed popularity in the late nineteenth century as the idea of secular progress, buttressed by scientific and technological discovery, thus reinforcing the idea that, by diligent application of sheer human effort and goodwill, ills and pains (that mortal flesh is heir to) would become things of the past. The thought was, roughly, that just as anesthesia had made the horrors of surgery obsolete, and shipbuilding technology had done the same for chancy, uncomfortable ocean voyages, modern social sciences would eradicate poverty and eradicate class distinctions. Psychology would eliminate neurotic terrors, it was thought, and pharmacology would wipe out disease. Science, broadly and popularly defined, would alleviate human misery. In mythic language, humanity would be able, by its own unassisted, innate genius, to find the way back to paradise.

That notion of general progress—the humanist vision—is by no means dead. But it has been counterbalanced by the experience of the twentieth century, which has shocked us back into the awareness that we have not found the way to paradise and that, quite possibly, our innate faculties have led us in the opposite direction.

---

15. The implications of this rather generous and noble-sounding sentiment were partly responsible for goading Socrates himself into philosophy. What Protagoras seemed to intend by this phrase was that ethical and moral standards are conventional, that whatever humans enforce as the moral code is the only moral code in existence, there being no objective and universal moral imperative as there are, for example, physical laws. This stark moral relativism Socrates intuited as the route to chaos.

– 4 –

A Natural Theology

God is a shout in the street.

—JAMES JOYCE, *ULYSSES*

We believe in one God, the Father,
the Almighty, maker of heaven and earth,
of all that is, seen and unseen.

—NICENE CREED

The first epigram for this chapter comes from Stephen Dedalus in the "Telemachus" episode of James Joyce's *Ulysses*. What he says is true. The word, or more properly the noise, pronounced "God" is probably heard most often as a shout in the street—an exclamation—than in any other way. People say "Oh, God!" almost reflexively, and not just when disaster strikes. Many habitually say it at the slightest negative provocation: "Oh, God, I forgot my keys." This is nothing new. In the early third century, the theologian Tertullian mentioned that uneducated pagans instinctively said "O God!" when surprised. Over the next twenty-four hours, note every use of the word *God* you hear and say yourself. Then categorize these uses, noting how often the word is used prayerfully, theologically, reflexively, profanely, and so on.

Profane use of some words may shock some well-meaning Christians, but the very fact of this use of the word *God* points to the strength behind that word (as does the even more powerful, and therefore more objectionable, use of the name "Jesus"; add the title "Christ" and the exclamation becomes downright morally offensive to all sorts of people).

Most people have probably been taught that such use is improper. It is a matter of manners for them. Some will have been taught this lesson more harshly, so that the name takes on the force of what Freud called a "taboo"—a forbidden word and powerful. But what is the reason for the word's power?

Asked why casual profane use of the word *God* is objectionable—when, after all, calling on God is something God seems to want—many pious people will claim it violates the third commandment, the prohibition on taking God's name in vain. The commandment seems to prohibit casual use of a word that should be used in a deliberate, ritual manner. But is "God" God's name?

Reflection will suggest that "God" is not God's name. The exclamation "Jesus Christ!" probably sounds more blasphemous to pious ears, because it *is* a name, and for Christians, God's name. *God* is not a proper noun. *God* in Old English, the oldest form of the language of which we have knowledge, was what language students call a "common noun." It pointed to a reality, but did not "name" a specific individual. It could be used to translate the neutral Latin word *deus*, which was no one's name.

But God does have a name. According to ancient Hebrew tradition it is "Yahweh," or at least the consonants of that word. (Ancient Hebrew was written with consonants only, so the vowels are an educated guess.) A thought-provoking summary of the possible early history of this name is available in Gerhard von Rad's *Theology of the Old Testament*. The name may originally have been a battle cry, von Rad writes, a natural sound related to "hurrah" and "Yah." Over time it became the sacred name, and the early Hebrews were convinced that God had shared the secret of God's name with them, through their patriarch Abraham. Another Old Testament tradition records that Moses first received the name. The Hebrews thus were privy to a secret and to an intimate relationship with God. One of the first steps in becoming friends in human relationship is the sharing of names. In contrast, one of the horrors of certain Kafka stories, and of certain modern films, is the scarcity or absence of names.

Whenever English Bibles in the Authorized tradition come upon the name "Yahweh"—as in Genesis 2:4 in the King James Bible—it is translated "Lord" and printed entirely in capital letters. This practice is usually explained as a concession to later Jewish tradition, which understood the name "Yahweh" as ineffable and included a taboo on its pronunciation. But given historical attitudes toward the Jews in England, this explanation seems less than likely.

More likely is that biblical translations avoid the name for the same reason later Judaism avoided it. It is too powerful. Some modern translations, such as the Jerusalem Bible, produced by Roman Catholic scholars, use the name freely, but descendants of the Authorized Version of 1611, such as the Revised Standard Version and its permutations, keep the ban.

After these considerations, the word *God* takes on aspects of a name. Many people do think of *God* as a proper name. Surely this accounts for the word's capitalization, a universal practice in English-speaking Christianity. By modern convention, this means the word is intended as a name, since, other than words beginning sentences, modern English capitalizes nothing but names. More significant, we address God in prayer as "God": "O God, make speed to save us."

Throughout the first section of the Catechism, we used the word *God* as a given, using it to explain humanity and human nature. We used the word without "defining" it, or discussing what is meant by it. This is not an illegitimate practice, as all dictionaries are, at bottom, circular, in that words are defined in terms of other words. Previous knowledge must be assumed. Remember that the word *red* is never defined, but you know what it means. Similarly, *God* is a primary word, as we have defined that term in the preface, and primary words are without definition in the verbal sense.

Yet even to an atheist, sentences in the first section of the Catechism would be intelligible. Though the atheist would judge them "false," he would likely not judge them "nonsense." This example is not so baffling, since we can talk about unicorns and make sense, though we agree they do not exist. Only a few modern philosophers, such as the early Wittgenstein, have said that such talk is nonsense since it has no real referent. Like everybody else, the atheist would have had a working definition of God as a (or the) "intelligent, conscious, purposeful being who created everything." This is far from the only historical definition of God. It does not suit Zeus, for example, nor a Hindu divinity, nor the Yahweh of early layers of the Old Testament. But our Judeo-Christian conditioning enables us to say that virtually all readers of the Catechism would have this definition in mind—especially since the document has not yet directed thought toward that God.

God the Father

Section 2 of the Catechism, "God the Father," does direct our attention toward God. As God comes into mental focus, what do we see?[1]

First is the assertion that what we claim to know about God the Father, or about God as revealed as Father, comes from the revelation to Israel as part of the set of books containing the Old Covenant, our Old Testament. This is not a gratuitous assertion but is as intentional as anything in the Catechism. One reason for the statement is to dispel any tendency toward a depreciation of our Hebraic heritage. Modern New Testament scholarship has bestowed a strong sense of the Jesus' Jewish background, but this is only a fraction of the reality contained in this assertion. The transcendent and monotheistic nature of Christianity is a direct offshoot of the stem which is Hebraism; no other religion could have produced us. Christianity began with the revelation to Israel, a sentient being conveying information to a subset of humanity and not to another subset. Any objective study of comparative religion will confirm that ethical monotheism—the belief in a single God vitally involved with, concerned for, and productive of the ethical life of humankind—is unique to the ancient Hebrews.

This is not to say that God did not reveal other aspects of God's reality to other peoples, nor does it rule out other systems of religious thought. The simple fact is that the Old Testament prophets were the first to claim—or to notice, intuit, or receive— that God cared deeply about human behavior. Buddha, in the same century as Isaiah, taught compassion, but not because the gods of the Hindu pantheon demanded it. Socrates taught intellectual integrity in spite of Zeus and his kin, not because of them. Confucius was a thoroughgoing Erastian. He thought, as did Cicero, that the value of theology was as a prop for a well-ordered state, a theory most articulated by the sixteenth-century Swiss theologian Thomas Erastus. Except for Erastus, all these individ-

---

1. I do not mean that we actually "picture" God, but that we have a mental concept of God. René Descartes carefully distinguishes "concepts" from "imaginings," and I follow his suggestion here.

uals were polytheists and believed in a multiplicity of authoritative supernatural powers, forces, intelligences, or persons.

These observations are all the more important in that Christian
theology parts company with Judaism most abruptly over the
doctrine of the Trinity, a unique teaching which we will explore
in depth. But prior to the Trinity comes Christian monotheism.
Our first revelation was that of Israel. So we, too, are ethical
monotheists, and the doctrine of the Trinity does not change that
we believe in one God.

Belief in one God hence is our first assertion, with the Catechism quoting the Creed. We may or may not believe in other
supernatural beings, such as angels, who are mentioned in Scripture but not in the Creed. While many Christians believe in angels,
we do not believe in any other being with the power, the ultimacy,
and the creative capacity of God. We do not believe with the polytheists that any other supernatural beings can have authoritative
power. We do not believe, with the Manicheans, in two equally
powerful, equally authoritative supernatural intelligences.[2]

At this point we still have not defined the word *God*. We have
taken the provisional position that *God* is one of the primary
words, undefinable in other terms, though we "know what it
means." Perhaps we should not define the word. To define means
literally "to set boundaries around," and God is without boundaries, infinite. An Aristotelian definition—which remains the
model for dictionary definitions—establishes the genus or larger
family for any reality, then distinguishes it from other members of
that genus by differentiae that specify its species. Western tradition deriving from Aristotle thus defines a human being, for example, as a "rational animal."[3] God, however, is unique. No other
beings are similar to God, so even using a word like *being* seems

---

2. Still, Christianity has borrowed from both polytheism and Manichaeism.
Polytheism has contributed to the Christian mythology of angels, while
Manichaeism has influenced the Christian understanding of personal evil as
expressed by the myth of Satan.

3. The previous chapter offers a theological alternative to this definition,
but not a contrary position. We understand "rationality" as a spiritual
attribute, albeit not the only such attribute, and probably not the defining
attribute, as modern rationalists beginning with Descartes maintained.

inappropriate. God is a single genus, and nothing else belongs to that genus. God thus is *sui generis*, a class alone.

All these statements are true, yet everything that follows in the Catechism and Creed "defines" God—not in the limiting sense of an Aristotelian definition, but by making positive assertions. An entire school of theology and spirituality, called the *apophatic* tradition, strictly denied that we could make such assertions. God, that tradition said, can be approached only by the *via negativa*, the "negative way" of denying positive assertions. God is not, for example, frail and fragmented, nor is God "great," since our word *great* refers only to human or other naturally occurring greatness, and God is supernatural. The classic example of this theological approach in English tradition is the fourteenth-century treatise *The Cloud of Unknowing*. The most authoritative Christian statement occurs in the work of Pseudo-Dionysius, the sixth-century mystical author of *Divine Names* and the *Celestial Hierarchy*.

While one must admit the integrity of the apophatic way and its usefulness in mysticism, the tradition makes one very dubious assumption—that human beings have no direct experience of God. The apophatic way therefore claims that humans' assertions about God are necessarily conditioned by the finite realities they have experienced. Obviously, the great practitioners of the negative way did not believe this claim. On the contrary, they often assert that they themselves have had experience of God. They are concerned, with Wittgenstein, with the limits of language in expressing encounters they believed were real.

Their theological position stands for us not as a deterrent but as a warning. Whatever we assert about God is analogical, and therefore partial. At every point we test the linguistic limits, and our attitude should reflect that awareness. The realization need not deter us, any more than it should deter us from trying to describe the color red or the taste of chocolate. At the same time, we should take comfort in the fact that serious thinkers, beginning with Aristotle, have attempted to define or describe God.

The influence of Aristotle is felt in the first assertion in the Nicene Creed. The first and second chapters of Genesis and the first phrases of the Fourth Gospel are also present, but less vividly.

Less theologically motivated than his teacher Plato, and more
determined to restrict himself to what he thought philosophy
should do—to contemplate human thought—Aristotle determined to begin all inquiry with sense impressions and to build
from there. Eventually, Aristotle himself became an authority, valued more for his conclusions than his approach. Therefore, when
thinkers in the sixteenth and seventeenth centuries returned to
Aristotle's own methods, as empiricists, they seemed to many to
be anti-Aristotelians. Even philosophers who began to distrust
sense impressions were not really invalidating Aristotle. Had Aristotle gone nearsighted, and realized it, he would not have trusted
his eyes. Like earlier thinkers, the pre-Socratic philosopher-scien-
tists whom Aristotle admired,[4] he was impressed with the phenomenon of change and the contradictory phenomenon of
permanence. One of his logical claims was that, since everything
is in motion,[5] and since no cause is apparent, there must be a
Prime Mover, First Mover, or Unmoved Mover—all labels
invented by Aristotelians and not by Aristotle—who starts the
process. This is a cleaner, more precise way of saying there must
be a reason for the complex cosmos, that it must be the product of
something intentional and intelligent.

This argument represents far less than the Christian theologian wants to say about God, but it has value for that reason. Aristotle was trying to determine what type of theology that human
reason, unaided by revelation or mythic imagination, could
develop. This was his answer, which Thomas Aquinas borrowed
almost without modification for his *Summa Theologiae*.

It is interesting to note the relative scarcity in theology of arguments for God's existence. Newcomers to the field often have
the impression that theology must spend a great deal of energy

---

4. So much, that he is our major source for what they said or wrote. More
fragments of the pre-Socratic thinkers appear in Aristotle's writings than
anywhere else.

5. "Motion" here is not quite the same thing as "movement," though we
use the terms synonymously. By motion we mean roughly what modern
physics means, which says that everything is "in motion" even when standing still. Thus, there is no such thing as stasis.

on the question of whether God exists, but that is untrue. The question of God's existence has always belonged more to philosophy, and to the division called metaphysics, which takes such basic questions as its subject. Theology by contrast generally assumes the existence of God. It is interested in conveying further information about God, roughly analogous to the literary genre of biography. Few biographies waste time establishing that their subject existed. But the analogy is rough, because many persons do doubt or deny the existence of God. Thus theology, which has an apologetic aspect, has from time to time invaded the territory of philosophy, and advanced arguments about God's existence.[6]

Some theologians regard such invasions as contemptible, and any argument for God's existence or application of native reason to theology as invalid. This was the position of the Swiss Protestant Karl Barth, who remains one of the most influential thinkers of the modern era. Barth denied the possibility of any knowledge of God through unaided human reason, of any "natural theology." Influenced by his reading of Rudolf Otto, who, in his *Idea of the Holy*, pointed to the utter transcendence of the otherness of God, by the Hebraic tradition, and by his understanding of St. Augustine, Barth tried to correct the modern tendency that exalted humanity and to restore the Pauline conviction of our utter dependence. Stated simply, Barth understood St. Paul, St. Augustine, and their many disciples to say that human reason, by virtue of the fall of humanity, is so corrupted as to be poisonous, so tainted with sin as to be blind. Contemporary research shows that this reading of Augustine is impossible, but Barth used it to restore a balanced anthropology. As we have suggested, the classic Christian view of humanity is paradoxical—on the one hand, humanity is the most exalted of species. On the other hand, it is

---

6. I use the word argument rather than the alternative proof, since the latter has for many people a connotation of conclusiveness that is inappropriate here. Actually, the word prove originally meant "to test, to try out," and is in that sense ideal for our use, but a "deductive proof" has come to mean something clinched by reasoning, and that as far as I know has not happened yet in this area.

the most debased. Barth intuited that the exaltation had proceeded too far, and that trust in human reason needed a balance. His conclusion for theology approaches the conclusions of the apophatic mystics. All we can say about God is negative, until the light of revelation comes. Like them, Barth stands as a warning, though we need not take him as a roadblock.

Related to the Prime Mover argument is the traditional *argument from design*. It too starts with the evidence of the senses—in this case, of a world of dazzling, even bewildering complexity. This is how the world appeared to Thomas Aquinas, who presents this argument most clearly. Nature seems immensely organized. It is only recently that a concept of entropy, of things tending toward disintegration and chaos, has begun to occur to human minds. Far more natural is the impression of organization, of extraordinary design. Again applying the axiom that existing conditions must have a cause, Thomas added the secondary consideration, that the cause is always more complex than the result. A man can produce a statue of a man, or a complex computer, but not a human body or human mind.[7] Therefore, there must be an intentional intelligence, a "divine craftsman," capable of the design we see, behind what we see.

These arguments underlie our creedal claims because they begin with the assertion of God's creativity. God, we imply by our Creed, is a being who creates—that is primary. God is in part our response to the fact that there *is* being. This question never troubled Aristotle apparently, but seized Aquinas, who said that God's essence is Being and that God shares that essence. In this discussion we are taking a position mapped by John Macquarrie in his *Principles*, and preceded by the traditional understanding of the divine Name as meaning "He Who Is," to borrow from Anglo-Catholic theologian E. L. Mascall.

We are also approaching the theology of the eleventh-century archbishop St. Anselm, who offered the classic ontological proof of the existence of God in his *Monologion*. Behind Tillich, Macquarrie, Heidegger, and all existentialist-oriented theology

---

7. Only in recent centuries have philosophers, beginning with David Hume, questioned this principle.

stands Anselm. God, according to Anselm's reasoning, is necessary being.[8] Others do not have to exist, but God does, and we have the proof in our own minds. We cannot imagine an ideal being without the attribute of existence; therefore, that being necessarily exists. Other theologians by and large accepted this proof until the seventeenth century. Since then, it has been tried and rejected repeatedly. Descartes revived it;[9] Immanuel Kant thought he had disproved it; Hegel reembraced it. The proof has since been resuscitated with Phoenix-like regularity.[10]

The ontological argument, and the theological ramifications of God's name, Yahweh, again are in a curious and perhaps surprising way reinforced by modern physical science. Our everyday sense of reality is earthbound. We are accustomed to dealing with matters on the scale in which we encounter them in the here and now. "Here" has turned out to be a limited fragment of the universe, "now" a subjective fragment of history. In our corner of the cosmos, it makes eminent sense to divide time and space, matter and action. Our languages, which all have nouns and verbs, reflect that this is the way things are.[11] But contemporary physics asserts that all these divisions are fictions. Time and space are the same thing, matter and action inseparable. The best science now understands what we have traditionally and intuitively called

---

8. Aquinas said the same thing later. Anselm is a unique figure of the early Middle Ages and the first of the great medieval thinkers.

9. Many would find Descartes' version as persuasive as Anselm's. The validity of either version, however, turns on the validity of the above principle, which states that an effect must be in some sense "less than" its cause. If this is not valid, then it is know valid to conclude from the effect—my idea of the existent God—the cause—the existent God.

10. The proof provoked a commonsense response from the monk Gaunilo, who, calling himself the Fool (the one who says there is no God), pointed out that the idea of a perfect island may be held in the mind, without there being such an island. Anselm replied that existence is not part of the perfection of an island, as it is of God.

11. The issue of reality and its relationship to language structures is a great concern of linguist Noam Chomsky, who asserts a Platonic-like sense of innate mental structures. Our argument is congruent with his thinking. We inhabit a portion of the universe in which it would make sense for intelligent creatures to develop, as part of evolution, mental mechanisms that reflect the local version of reality.

"matter" to be an "event"—a happening, a motion of energy in time, a verb. This is almost inconceivable. It is also exactly what a God whose name is Yahweh might be expected to create.

None of these arguments is explicit in any creed. Arguments are catechetical, not symbolic. Nor are they, as we have suggested, near the center of theological concerns. But they do underlie our assertions, in that we do posit the existence of God. We "believe in" God in many ways, but that belief begins with trust in the existence itself. The moral argument that Aquinas offered may be most compelling today. It is the approach often taken by modern apologists like G. K. Chesterton and C. S. Lewis, and it may speak to us most powerfully because of the acute ethical questions raised by the twentieth century.[12] The argument states that, just as the apparent design of the world must originate somewhere, so must the innate moral sense of human beings.[13] Even without cultural conditioning, human beings seem to have a moral sense separate from natural instincts that it can, even in very young children, counter and oppose the natural instinct. In brief, the argument runs, that moral instinct must be the intent of the ethical God we read about in the Old Testament, the God of the levitical codes and the prophetic consciousness.

From the existence of God—from the statement "I believe in God," which can be uttered in good conscience by most of humanity—to the next assertion is a quantum leap. The next assertion, so familiar that most of us do not notice it, is that God is Father. This word is controversial for new philosophical reasons, which are not, despite the complaints of certain traditionalists, ephemeral and faddish, but serious and instructive. In the past, calling God "Father" was not a stumbling block. It was accepted as part of Christianity. Now it is a major stumbling block, and not

---

12. This century has simultaneously raised the theological challenge of theodicy—the justification of belief in God, at least in a good God, in the face of obvious injustice and human suffering. Theodicy raises the classic question of "bad things happening to good people" with a vividness which is possibly unprecedented. We shall return to this matter in the final chapter.

13. We shall return to this issue when we approach the Commandments, since it is germane there as well.

just in the Creed but in the faith itself, which has uncritically accepted the word. The controversy it now stirs is valuable insofar as it forces us to examine the word, to find its value.

The Catechism inserts the word "loving" before Father to show, in the words of the explanation, that "[the universe] is the work of a single loving God." Here the catechetical mode is demythologizing the symbol Father. Why?

As with the Divine Name, historical context may prove helpful. Given that Genesis may be seen, from one angle, as a "demythologized" version of the cosmological story, nowhere is that more true than regarding the "fatherhood" of God. The concept is anathema to what Genesis is trying to do. In fact, God is never called "father" in Genesis. Throughout the rest of the Old Testament, use of the word remains rare, contrary to popular impressions.

By contrast, father-gods abound in other Middle Eastern mythologies which are in many respects parallel to Genesis. These myths invariably involve the sexual production of the cosmos, local variations on the universal theme of sky-god impregnating mother-earth with the seminal fluid, which is rain.[14] Genesis, as modern biblical scholars have shown, demythologizes this tale. For the first time God is transcendent, separate from creation. In fact, the Judeo-Christian God is the least gender-bound of any deity and is beyond human characteristics. God is not "male," except by metaphor. Yahweh does not create by using sex organs, as do other gods. Yahweh creates by speech, which is common to males and females. Yahweh does not mate, has no divine consort and no human mistresses. Recent investigations pointing out that the male god had a divine consort in Hebrew myths before Genesis prove nothing except that the version we have is demythologized. Yahweh is not a man on any level. Finally, the first active verb in Genesis, and the second statement about God, pictures God in feminine, not masculine, terms, as the "divine wind sweeping over the waters." *Wind* is a feminine noun in Hebrew. God the Father was

14. This is the sort of religion that scandalized certain of our Christian forebears, most recently the Victorians.

not present during the primeval creation, despite the claims of later centuries.

If all this is true, why is God called Father? Perhaps the reason, to paraphrase T. S. Eliot, is that humankind can stand only so much demythologization. The concept of God as Father reappears in later Scripture.[15] Yet a clear reading of the Old Testament will reveal other images of God, some wonderful and unexpected, and the Father image, as I have suggested, displays no primacy before the New Testament. This primacy of God as Father occurs despite, and not because of, the negative patriarchal connotations. The Catechism suggests this fact as well. The word *father* implied responsibility, closeness, intimacy, similarity in kind, intelligence of superior degree, priority, protectiveness, and a love expressible in no other way. The word *mother*, though valid in biblical terms, wherein the femininity of God is substantially represented, was too associated with sexual myths and attempts to define the term more broadly. But, despite attempts to create an inclusive definition, the word *father* is "exclusive" in the sense in which Protestant theologian Sallie McFague uses the term. It excludes too many persons on the basis of their experience, and in this sense it excludes many males as well as females. As Paul Tillich insists, even the most time-honored symbols can become idols when elevated to a status they do not deserve. Perhaps theology has been guilty of idolatry regarding the word *father*.

But even this trend is changing. The previously mentioned principle of *lex orandi, lex credendi* shows something interesting. Believers are increasingly feeling free to address "God our Mother" or the like without feeling in theological jeopardy. No one may yet call God "Yahweh," but many are beginning to call upon God as "Mother." This renaming has proved disturbing to traditionalists, but the practice harkens to Isaiah, who expresses God's femininity and motherhood more consistently than any other biblical author.

---

15. By "later," I do not imply that Genesis is the oldest book, but that it was handed down, and written down, before the books that develop the Fatherhood concept.

In the preceding paragraph I use the term *traditionalists*. That word must be qualified. There is no monolithic Judeo-Christian tradition, but only an impression of one—the product of selective cultural memory. The tradition is, rather, multifaceted. Within that tradition we find such powerfully, unequivocally female[16] images of God as that of Isaiah 42:14, "now I will cry out like a woman in travail" (RSV). As Elizabeth A. Johnson writes, "[T]ravail is a not inconsequential part of female life. Women's experience of suffering the world over includes the pain attending labor and childbirth, the penalty incurred for freely chosen actions for justice, the sorrow of grief over harm that comes to others, and the destruction known in personal degradation."[17] Insofar as the tradition has consistently portrayed God as suffering,[18] woman can serve as *imago Dei*.

It is significant here that the Catechism explains a term by substituting another word for it. This is highly unusual in the catechetical form. Normally, the Catechism expands words into phrases and phrases into paragraphs; it is discursive where the Creed is condensed. The word substitution suggests the powerful problems involved with the word *father*. At the same time, it reminds us of the equally powerful reality at work. Our cultural context makes us more sensitive to the weakness and inadequacy of the word *father* and, at the same time, directs our attention to aspects of God's reality we might otherwise have missed had we, like our forebears in the faith, accepted it as a healthy way of relating to and addressing God.

One of the negative connotations of fatherhood is the idea of might makes right, that the strongest figure in the family or clan has the most authority regardless of intelligence, moral power, and so on. This leads appropriately into our consideration of the next term: *almighty*. What is intended by the word *almighty* is best approached through history. The word connotes many ideas in

---

16. I deliberately avoid the word feminine.

17. Elizabeth A. Johnson, *She Who Is* (New York: Crossroad, 1992), p. 254.

18. The paradox involved in portraying God as both suffering and impassible, transcendent and immanent, will be addressed in the final chapter. That God is often portrayed as having feelings, as not being transcendent, is undeniable, and the only point germane to the issue.

English, most having to do with strength or power. We think usually of the mightiest men as the strongest physically. The "mightiest nation" usually refers to the nation with the most military strength. Any other use of the word seems to derive from this meaning. If we speak, for example, of a nation's "economic might" or a person's "mighty spirit," we already seem to be speaking metaphorically. *Might* is an old and simple word, its meaning physical and straightforward. Our use of the word has retained that characteristic through the centuries.

It is, however, not an exact translation of the word in the Nicene Creed. The creedal word is *pantokratora*, which consists of two root words: *pan*, meaning "all" (as in panacea, "cure-all"), and *krat-*, from the verb meaning "to rule." The same root exists in *democracy*, which means "rule by the people," and related words like *autocrat* and *aristocrat*. Therefore, "all-ruling" would have been a better translation, and might have been used if the Creed had not first been translated into Latin, which substituted the word *omnipotens*—which really does mean "almighty."

Thus the original idea was not that God is the strongest being, leading to questions such as, "Can God make a rock he cannot lift?" The statement was meant to mean that God has dominion everywhere, that there is no part of the universe for which God is not responsible, of which God is not aware, for which God does not have concern as well as authority. Perhaps the simplest way to put this is that the "all" in *almighty* refers not to the might itself, but to its object, the cosmos. It is not that God's strength is unlimited in degree, but in scope.

For the ancients, this was itself a novel claim. Pagan religion thought of various gods as having fields of jurisdiction, as in the myth in which Zeus, Poseidon, and Hades, the sons of Ouranos, divide the universe into sky, sea, and underworld for their dominions. The Romans were if anything more diversified in their theology. Numinous beings were responsible for such domestic realities as hearth and cupboard, for fountains and wells, as well as for families, cities, and so on. Middle Eastern *panthea*, which provide the context for Old Testament Hebraism, were similarly diverse, and less rationally ordered than these classical counterparts.

To the early Hebrews, the concept of a God unlimited in scope was strange. Yahweh was their God, but that did not suggest that other tribes and nations lacked gods. Evidence appears in Old Testament language proclaiming Yahweh "a great king above all Gods" (cf. the Venite, Book of Common Prayer, 82). The Old Testament on the whole is not monotheistic; other gods exist. It was not until the time of the prophets in the sixth century that the concept of a single god, and a universal single god, a *Pantokrator*, began to seize the imaginations of a few daring persons.

It is, in other words, the second great guarantor of monotheism in the Creed, and thus something far more powerful than unlimited strength. It was a challenge in the fourth century A.D., when the Creed was assembled, since the great majority of people still believed in a pantheon. The notion of one God remains a challenge in this postmodern world. Here I am concerned not so much with what people think, or profess to think, but with the imagination, a serious and often underrated factor in theological experience. Most people claim to be theists of one sort or another. Most Americans, if polled, claim to be Christians, though what they really mean is "gentiles." Whatever this conscious claim means, most do not accept a *Pantokrator* God. Most limit the jurisdiction of God to a narrow range of reality—occasional worship; crisis moments such as serious sickness and danger; moments of great expectation such as death, marriage, and birth; and selected, scattered religious observances such as Easter. The ethical conviction that God is vitally concerned with the marketplace or politics is not there. God has no place in these arenas in most people's imagination.

To some readers, this statement will be self-evident. Others will resist. For the latter, I ask them to imagine an executive of some enormous moneymaking concern, a computer company or auto manufacturer. Imagine that she or he is also a hard-working vestry member in an affluent parish—not a bad person by any stretch. Now, imagine that person making a decision not based on the "best interests," that is, economic interests, of the company, but on prophetic ethics—not making a public issue of it, telling no one, but actually basing a business decision on theology.

Can you imagine that happening? Probably not. I cannot. In fact, the sketch seems bizarre. As we think through this fictional case together, a voice inside us says, "This is ridiculous. Nobody in the real, practical world acts like that, or should act like that." That voice limits God's authority. If the voice affects you and me, who are doing theology, how loud is it elsewhere? The putative executive of our imagination does not lack ethics. The executive does not use imagination to extend God's jurisdiction to this arena of life. He or she would think it odd, irrational, or unhealthy to think this way.

But *almighty* means that God's authority is unlimited, not that God is stronger than we are. God *is* stronger than we are, but so are blue whales, hurricanes, and angels. God holds sway over every detail of our lives related to business, sex, recreation, and bodily function, as well as over the details of the vestry meeting behind the Gothic church facade. It is difficult for most of us to acknowledge God's authority in these areas. It is easy to substitute another authority, another god.

The words *maker* or *creator* (the Book of Common Prayer uses the former for the Nicene Creed, the latter in the Apostles' Creed) raise less controversy than *almighty*, but they also conceal a conceptual richness. Behind the word *maker* lies the Greek word from which "poet" comes. Out of all the available words for artist or craftsman, the councils chose the word that suggests that God created worlds the way poets create poems. This seems highly appropriate given a God who speaks things into existence. We ourselves become elements in a cosmic poem or, as Dante saw, personae in a comedy.[19]

We have already touched briefly on the problem of creativity. The concept of creation ex nihilo was made explicit later, by St. Augustine, for example, and by the Scholastic tradition that followed him, but here it is implicit. To create implies to make something entirely new, something that did not exist previously in any form. It is the opposite or producing something from

---

19. Dante uses the word *comedy* in the classical rather than the modern sense. His *Commedia* is not a comic poem, but rather a poem whose drama is resolved in a positive way.

assembly, but is the creativity expressed mythologically in the first chapter of Genesis.

Creativity is also implicit in the two all-inclusive phrases which follow in the original Nicene Creed: "of all things, visible and invisible." The phrases rule out preexistent stuff out of which God molds things into shape, which is the version presented in Genesis 2. Most probably have imagined creation of the second kind, God shaping and fashioning humankind out of dust or mud, or sculpting figures from rock. From the myth of Pygmalion and Galatea to the story of Frankenstein, this is the human image of creation. There is always a preexistent substance, some *hylē* (Greek for "matter"), which is "there," unexplained, from which to create. But because God shares being with us, we believe in creation ex nihilo—that something came from nothing.

The enigmatic world of modern science here makes an unanticipated contribution. Most know that physics posits an expanding universe that is part of the big bang theory, which most physicists accept as the working hypothesis for creation. The theory leads, however, to a problem and a solution which are less well-known. An expanding universe is becoming less dense, yet we know through measurable data that the universe remains constant in its density. The solution physics has offered and which physicists have accepted with no apparent shock is that matter is constantly being created—ex nihilo. Not matter "converted" from some other state, not matter imported from some other place, but matter created. The actual mass of the matter is known, as is its rate of appearance. This data amounts to empirical evidence for the fact of creation. Nothing like it has ever been known to humankind. The only reason I can give for physics' unflappable acceptance is that the postmodern scientific world had already inured them to wonder. For those who believe in a God who creates everything seen and unseen, the finding should be a source of tremendous affirmation and genuine joy.

Thus God's two chief attributes, according to the creedal claims, are universal authority and universal creativity, learned through the revelation to Israel. God's love, expressed through the same revelation, was not, in other words, the first attribute revealed, though this does not diminish its importance. If again we think of God in personal terms, this sequence makes sense. The first impressions we have of a human being may have to be modified later, but they are only "false" if that person is particularly deceptive or if our senses mislead us.[20]

"Of heaven and earth" was not in the original Nicene Creed but was the first expansion at the Council of Constantinople in 390. It is a mythic variation on what had already been affirmed. If God creates everything that is, seen and unseen, this God must have created heaven and earth. But the phrase is extremely valuable for its connotations. "Heaven and earth" resonates as a peculiarly all-inclusive phrase, encompassing for early humanity the known and the unknown. That the phrase still has that value is suggested by Raphael's painting *Academy at Athens*, wherein Plato points to the heavens and Aristotle to the earth to suggest their respective philosophical starting points. In the Greek, "heaven" is *ouranos*, the sky-father, the fierce and formidable creator of gods. To assert that Yahweh-God created *ouranos* is to show God's totality as creator in a deliberately mythic way, which has been lost in translation but was definitely there for the first people of the Creed.

The phrase "seen and unseen" covers everything, and that is its intent. Practically speaking, it means that God does not create only physical realities. God is also creator of the spiritual world, or, for those who prefer a less religious word, the psychological. God creates human emotions as surely as God creates clouds and grass. Just as the sheer extent of God's authority is stressed by the word *Pantokrator*, so is God's extensive creativity stressed in this phrase. The imagination of most people needs this challenge. It is easy for theistic people to conceive of God as the creator of a sunset or an attractive child, but God is also the creator of anger, sexual desire, and frustration. We are conditioned to think of

---

20. It is important to realize that the attributes of authority and creativity are not contradictory to subsequent attributes. That these attributes came prior to the attributes of love and mercy deluded many in the past into a dichotomy between an Old Testament God of justice and a New Testament God of mercy—a reprehensible misimpression. An interesting historical variant, or perhaps the logical extreme, can be found in the idiosyncratic mythology of William Blake.

these things as "bad," but theologically they are not. They can be raw materials for good, though they may prove otherwise. They, like humans, are not created bad.[21]

The explanation to the Creed affirms "that the universe is good." This is far more than a jejune phrase or wishful thinking, but is somewhat counterintuitive. The perspective of recent history, compounded by the Western Christian tradition, has tended to distort our vision, which is understandable. The perspective leads us into such everyday statements as "everything is ruined" or "all is lost." It leads also to human doctrines of pessimism such as that of the modern historian Oswald Spengler in the magnificently depressing *Decline of the West*, or to the doctrines of the Cynics. The universe, on the whole, is good. Human imperfection—sin—has distorted our view of reality, like the desert nomad who assumes the entire world is arid and hot. The Creed is meant to be repeated often, because we need to remind ourselves regularly of this cosmic perspective that the world is good, on the whole.

God is said to sustain and direct as well as to create, and all three verbs are in the present tense. One value of the creation stories expressed as myth in our scriptural tradition is that myth is timeless. Myth happens in mythic time, not in clock time, and therefore the stories should not be read as part of a rational historical past. Nothing in the Genesis account implies that creation is "finished." From early in Christian tradition—the earliest mention is in the Letter of Barnabas, written in the early second century—it has been asserted that God begins creation anew on the great Eighth Day, the Lord's Day, the Eschatological Day. Creation is happening this second. Your mind, as it accepts, rejects, or modifies what you are reading, is part of that process.[22]

All these ideas stand in opposition to Deism, another theology with an apparently timeless appeal. Deism was the preeminent

---

21. On this point Aristotle was clear. Despite being a realist and empiricist, he states that nonmaterial things also exist, that they have matter and form, potentiality and existence.

22. The latest astrophysical discovery is that the universe may be accelerating in its expansion. Until 1998 the cosmological model depicted an expanding universe that was slowing in its expansion. It seems that it is not only growing more vast but is growing at an increasing rate.

theological philosophy of the eighteenth century, the age of the Enlightenment. Among the outstanding tenets of Enlightenment thought was the idea that reality is, ultimately, explicable in rational, even mathematical, terms. The seventeenth-century philosophers had adumbrated this development, but the Enlightenment raised it to a first principle. The simultaneous invention by Isaac Newton and Gottfried Leibniz of calculus supported the idea, since calculus was able to solve problems in physics that had been elusive. These problems, such as the acceleration of rapidly moving objects, had endured since Euclid and had been considered impossible to solve mathematically. With calculus, Newton was able to construct a new physics which seemed, for the moment, to have the potential for explaining everything, at least anything that existed in mathematics. This possibility carried with it the idea of a comprehensive philosophy.

A completely mechanistic model of the universe—a clockwork universe—seemed possible. Closer to our time, Newton's system proved inadequate as the field of vision of science expanded, raising new problems solved in part by twentieth-century physicists Niels Bohr, Albert Einstein, Max Planck, and Werner Heisenberg. But Newton seemed to have spoken the last word for the eighteenth century. As Alexander Pope said, "God said, 'Let Newton be,' and all was light."

It was in France, however, that the Age of Reason flourished to the fullest extent. The newly organized Académie Francaise was dedicated to the rational, scientific, and rational solution of any human problem. France even experimented briefly, in the immediate aftermath of her revolution, with an entirely materialistic, mechanistic political system, which "demythologized" human life to an unprecedented extent. Even the names of the months were changed to be "rational" instead of "mythical."

The latent destructive potential of these trends was realized soon enough. Antirational reactions in the arts, philosophy, political science, and religion soon appeared. But for our purposes it is important to realize what a heady, exhilarating atmosphere all this change represented. As Wordsworth, a democratic rationalist in his youth, wrote later, to be young then was "very heaven."

Heaven itself seemed to change during the Age of Reason. Instead of an immanent God, intimately involved with the created world, the rationalists invented a remote God, close in many ways to Aristotle's abstract Mover—a God who, to use their most famous image, created the world like a clock maker, winding it up and then leaving it to run on its own. The laws of physics provided the example of the mechanism that God had created. These laws, and not God, kept the cosmos, the megaclock, running on time.

The Enlightenment was displaced by the Romantic revolution, as the rationalist dream mutated overnight into the Reign of Terror, which followed the political revolution in France. The value of nonrational aspects of human experience reasserted itself with a vengeance. This renewal occurred in philosophy as strongly as in any facet of culture. Hegel gave eighteenth-century rationalism its most severe criticism in his *Philosophy of History*, and Immanuel Kant attempted to draw the limits of reason in his philosophical *Critiques*. But we remain, nevertheless, partial heirs of the Enlightenment. The French experiment failed, but the New World experiment, the United States, proved successful on an unprecedented scale, setting up an entirely new nation on the principles of British rationalism. We are children of the Enlightenment, as surely as we are also Romantics.

Both movements affect our theology. The clock-maker God did not disappear. This is the model of God many people, including many who would not even recognize the Deist label, have developed in their unconscious. Many believe in a creator God, a transcendent God, but not in a sustaining and directing presence. Often, these theists misunderstand the Christian vision of God as involving God's occasional "intervention" in the created world in the form of miracles, which are exceptions to God's normal detachment. Such misunderstanding is opposed to the genuine Christian tradition, which understands God as always immanent and transcendent. In other words, theists tend to project their Deism onto other theologies, so strongly do they experience Deism. The medieval philosopher might have said that this is to be expected. Natural theology can lead the mind to the understanding of God expressed in Deism, but no further.

The Creed explicitly rejects the divine clock maker. The Judeo-Christian God not only creates, but also sustains and directs. God also "loves" God's creation. The parent image is eloquent here. Like a good father, God not only begets but also raises the offspring. The gender in this case is unimportant. It could be argued that the image of the mother might work better, in that the mother often tends to be more "parental" than the father. Whether this is due to biological instinct or to cultural reinforcement is the debatable point.

These considerations lead directly to the next catechetical matter. What do these thoughts reveal about "our place in the universe"? The first part of the creedal answer—"the world belongs to its creator"—sets up what will follow, which is a definition of our relationship to the rest of creation. Because God "owns" creation, or, better, because creation belongs to God the way a child belongs to its parents, any authority over creation given to humans consists of stewardship, not ownership.

An owner can do whatever the owner wishes, legally, with what belongs to him or her. Theoretically, you can put this book down, haul furniture outside, and chop it to bits. You cannot do this in the library or in someone else's home, or if your furniture is borrowed or leased. To do so would be dangerous, legally, to you, though the same action is involved as in the first example. All these considerations transfer to our relationship to the world.

The second part of the catechetical answer, that "we are called to enjoy [the created world] and care for it," may sound at first like a retreat from the English-speaking tradition, which used the word *dominion* in this context. The Authorized Version of 1611, for example, translates Genesis 1:26: "Let them have dominion over" the rest of creation. That word, for us, connotes power, even the cruel power which accompanies brutal disregard. Perhaps this is because the word was used in the past to justify domination of everything from trees to other primates to female spouses.

The word originally conjured a different image. It comes from the Latin *domus*, meaning "home." When the Authorized Version mentioned humankind's dominion over nature, it meant that this species was head of the household, loving, parental, responsible, and concerned. Reckless exploitation of natural resources or ruthless abuse of other species would be like a man who burns his own floorboards for firewood, or who roasts his dog for dinner—criminal, insane, or both.

The word *dominion* lost its root connotations. That is why, in its explanation, the Catechism is careful to use instead the positive words "enjoy" and "care for"—words that could be used of healthy parents and that *dominion* connoted in 1611. Now its connotations are sinister and horribly misleading. A better word might be cultivation, which denotes authority and power but also more positive connotations such as responsibility, affection, cooperation, and respect.

The verb *enjoy* still may come as a surprise. The word sounds odd in religion often associated with gloom and fallenness. In fact, the Judeo-Christian tradition all along has been world-affirming. The expulsion from the garden did not poison the rest of the world. Just because pain and suffering enter the world enjoyment and pleasure do not exit. Throughout the rest of the Old Testament, earthly pleasure is never criticized in and of itself, but is only wrong when enjoyed at the expense of others (see, e.g., Habakkuk 2). Even such humble, physical pleasures as a drink of cool water (as David experiences in *Kings*), rest, a bath, and a simple meal are celebrated. Any honest reading of the Bible will gain a positive estimate of deeper human pleasures, such as the exhilaration of natural beauty (Psalm 104) and of sex (Song of Songs).

The tradition, moreover, does not "permit" these pleasures, like a school principal who permits the breaking of the dress code on Fridays but would rather not have the dress code broken. The biblical words are commands, imperatives. We are called to enjoy the world.

We are to enjoy creation as God enjoys it. Otherwise, what would God mean by pronouncing it "good"? Like God, we are to exercise responsibility as well: we are to "care for" creation. There is continuity before and after the fall since, according to the myth, Adam and Eve still have "dominion." They still have to work the soil, name the animals, and so on after leaving the Garden. No one says that the initial agreement is canceled. Caring for creation has become more difficult, but not impossible.

Finally, we are to enjoy and care for the rest of the world "in accordance with God's purposes." This brings the catechetical answer full circle. We began by admitting that the world is God's; we admit that God has given us stewardship rights and duties; and we understand these rights and duties on God's terms. This is a simple but subtle concept, its implications easier to see if we consider what it means to enjoy the world. The negative impression enjoyment of the world conjures for many religious persons is not merely faulty theology. They notice a danger to enjoyment, but their slight error sends them into the Puritan mistake. In and of itself, enjoyment is a powerful capacity in a rational, spirited, and fleshly being. Our capacity for enjoyment is great. A great deal of harm can be traced, in part or entirely, to satisfaction of that capacity. Freud called this quest for satisfaction the pleasure principle, and, from the point of view of classic theology, he was absolutely correct.

We will examine this phenomenon in more detail when we consider the category of sin, since the distortion of enjoyment often is a factor in that reality. For now, we might observe that enjoyment of the world can take physical, intellectual, and spiritual forms, congruent with our advanced development in all three areas. When enjoyment does not accord or harmonize with the heart, with God's purpose, it becomes harmful. Such distortions range from addiction on the one hand to the inability to pursue long-term goals because of the need for delay of gratification on the other. Enjoyment of the world has led to limitless misery. Judeo-Christianity, a term used deliberately to express the single tradition of Judaism and Christianity (see below), acknowledges that fact and seek to understand it.

The current Book of Common Prayer is a remarkably consistent and comprehensive work, perhaps more than any previous edition. Its ability to answer questions about the implications of theology for human life provides an example of the consistency. In its renewed emphasis on the practice and the theology of baptism, the Church demonstrates the primacy of that sacrament with renewed purpose. Its full ethical implications are spelled out in the baptismal covenant, an aspect of covenant theology that we will examine shortly.

"All people are worthy of respect and honor, because all are created in the image of God, and all can respond to the love of God." The Ten Commandments address theological, then ethical concerns. The Catechism here, like the Creed, connects them. Our ethical duties, our duties toward one another as human beings, are based on a theological principle: that God's image is in us.

This is important. Ethical principles are not merely absolute and arbitrary, not merely "given" as sometimes viewed, but can be reasonably interpreted. Such interpretation represents part of the Christian response to a classic problem in ethical thought: Is an action good because God commands it, or does God command an action because it is good? Plato raises this question in the *Euthyphro*. The story of Abraham and Isaac treats it parabolically. The nineteenth-century philosopher-theologian Søren Kierkegaard meditates upon it in *Fear and Trembling*. The Christian response connects the goodness of a human act with the image of the divine within, thus short-circuiting the problem, showing it to be a false way of stating the question. God's command and good action are inseparable.

The words *respect* and *honor* are precise and deliberate. Christian tradition has, from time to time, dwelt on the degrees of honor due various beings. God deserves worship, the saints and the virgin Mary a little less than worship, and so on down the great chain of being. These reflections appealed to the sensibilities of a more hierarchically conscious age like the European Middle Ages, and do not appeal as greatly to us. In this context, however, the levels of honor make sense. God deserves worship; other creatures deserve our "care." Fellow humans deserve honor and respect.

Both *honor* and *respect* are Latin words. *Honor* in Latin means essentially what it means in English, emphasizing the public aspect of sincere regard. *Respect* is more curious. It comes from two words meaning, originally, "to look back" or "to look again"—to reconsider something that one has passed by. This is an eloquent explanation, for we respect others because they are worth "another look." Familiar with humanity because it is our identity and milieu, we do not notice our own supernatural value until we give it this second look, this respect. What we then notice, what we see, is the image of God. Usually sullied with the grim cast of life, it is there nonetheless.

The words *honor* and *respect* are, however, milder than some might have expected. Why are we not asked to "love" our fellow human being at this point? Love is, after all, stronger than respect. It is a biblical injunction, woven into our consciousness by the very document we are examining. Are not all people worthy of love because all are created in the image of God?

They are. But an enormous difficulty with the word *love*, which we have briefly encountered, is its breadth of meaning. We say, "I love my old shoes," "I love my house," "I love my dog," "I love my friend," "I love my daughter," "I love my spouse," "I love my religion," "I love my country," and "I love my God." These are nine easily distinguished things. Which sense of the word do we use if we say we should "love our fellow humans"? We shall have to admit that none of the above meanings fits precisely, and that some are dangerously misleading.

The word *love* will be useful, but not yet. It will be useful when we define it, and we shall define it when we have been reminded what it means. As in the case of sin, we avoid the more potent word. In this case, avoidance prevents two possible misunderstandings at opposite extremes. To be commanded to "love one's neighbor" or one's fellow human can sound too facile. Anyone can show love if all we mean is the vague and harmless affection we feel for worn-out automobiles or our hometown. Love can seem too difficult, by contrast, if we understand the powerful, self-sacrificing, painful yet joyous feeling of certain humans for others: David for Jonathan, Tristram for Isolde, Tony for Maria, Lear for Cordelia. This also is "love," but it is rare and by definition exceptional. It therefore cannot be commanded.

Most would mistake *love* in a theological work for the second type of love. To say that all are worthy of love in this sense would be nearly meaningless, like commanding humans to develop back muscles to the point where we could fly. It is not theoretically possible, and so it violates the essential practicality of the Catechism. *Respect* and *honor*, on the other hand, are difficult but by no means impossible. Further, they are not emotions, and, unlike love, can be commanded. It is possible to respect or honor anyone, given enough attention and will. As the origin of the word *respect* suggests, the question is one of attention.

"How was this revelation handed down to us?"

The Catechism now changes direction, setting up the next section. The answer provides, however, another example of the comprehensiveness we have seen throughout. We are about to turn our attention to the Old Covenant, as the Book of Common Prayer has turned our attention in worship to that covenant. Dramatically and practically, the Book of Common Prayer has restored, after centuries of omission, the Old Testament lesson to its position as the first reading for the principal Eucharist on the Lord's Day. I mean "centuries" quite literally. Not since the times of the earliest Church have Old Testament lessons been so prominently featured.

This is part of a recapturing, a restoration, of our rootedness in Judaism. I have deliberately been employing the unusual expression *Judeo-Christianity* to express this sense of a single tradition, as opposed to the adjective *Judeo-Christian*, which implies the combination of two traditions. This sense of monolithic tradition has been carefully introduced into the Catechism. Every belief we assert until the fifth question on page 849 of the Book of Common Prayer has come to us through our Hebraic ancestry. We hold every bit in common with contemporary Judaism.

Conversely, we have said not one sentence—except for a few illustrations deliberately borrowed from as wide a range of human experience as possible—that needs New Testament revelation. The first five sections of the Catechism, twenty-eight questions accounting for over 25 percent of the whole, could be expressed easily without reference to Christianity. We are confessing our Hebraic identity as never before.[23]

---

23. Some have labeled this identity as our "Jewishness," which is valid as long as we recognize that Judaism is a flourishing contemporary faith which had its origins at roughly the same time as Christianity. "Hebraic identity" is not identical with the Hebraism of the Old Testament, a term I have avoided out of respect for that religion and to avoid confusion. The key to Judaism is the Talmudic tradition. According to the Jewish saying, Torah without Talmud is not Judaism. This is true since Christianity can have Torah without Talmud.

Thus we assert, "This revelation was handed down to us through a community created by a covenant with God." One obvious aspect of that revelation is its communal aspect. This is highly significant, and separates this response from other interpretations of Christianity. Although we believe that God acts through individuals, we assert strongly that God typically has handed down revelation through communities, among these Israel and the New Israel. There is tension between the two modes of revelation, for the individual sometimes seems to bear God's word against the community, as in the case of the prophets, Jesus, and many reformers and mystics. The norm, however, is that revelation is passed through the community. When the community refuses the message, God chooses the individual messenger.

What is meant by a covenant with God?

First, what is meant by a covenant in general? A covenant is a relationship formed between individuals, between an individual and a group, or between groups. The Bible refers to covenants of all sorts. First Samuel 18:3, for example, tells of Jonathan making one with David. It is not, in other words, exclusively a theological term.

A covenant often occurs between unequal parties. When Jonathan makes this covenant with David, for example, they are not equals. Jonathan, as the king's son, has more power than David in the history. Covenants imply equality nonetheless. Two absolutely unequal parties cannot make covenants, although they may have relationships. We are related to the earth, but we cannot speak of "making a covenant with the earth," except in a figure of speech. It might make sense, however, to speak of the earth and the moon as having made a covenant. This is no less accurate or scientific than saying that their relationship is based on the "law" of gravity, since neither really obeys laws.

In any unequal covenant, the greater party initiates. Thus God initiates covenants with us, and we "respond in faith." For God to initiate a covenant moves us much nearer to God than we would be without such covenants. All other biblical covenants are between beings of the same species. That should not be overlooked. It is an extraordinary privilege for any group of humans to enter a covenantal relationship with the creator God.

The Old Covenant, then, is the "one given by God to the Hebrew people." The word *Old* has led to a great deal of misunderstanding in the past. Christians have treated it as if it meant "obsolete," as if it had been annulled. St. Paul even speaks this way on occasion in his letters.

Nothing about the "new" covenant implies that the "old" is therefore rescinded. Indeed, *old* can imply "worthy of veneration and respect," and it implies priority. These attitudes have been reinforced recently by the recovery of Old Testament consciousness we have just examined. The new attitudes suggest a sense in which the Old Covenant is still operative, still important, even for us. An Old Testament consciousness guards against the tendency in Christianity to denigrate the older aspects of the Judeo-Christian tradition, a tendency nearly as old as the faith itself. By the second century, the renegade Christian Marcion was already attempting to reject the Old Testament as the work of an alien and inferior God whom the new revelation had displaced.

The word *Hebrew* is to be distinguished from *Israelite* and *Jew*. Properly, its only synonym is *Israel* or *child of Israel*. *Israelite* and *Jew* are both too modern in that there were Hebrews before there were either Jews or Israelites. The latter term refer to a Hebrew after the settlement in ancient Palestine; thus, Moses was not an Israelite. The former term refers to the postdiaspora religion, the religion of the descendants of the Hebrews after the destruction of the Temple by the Roman army in 70 A.D.; thus, Abraham was not a Jew. Sometimes the words are used interchangeably, but this is a source of confusion.

More confusion, and of a more substantial sort, has been the result of the promise God made to the Hebrews. God promised "that they would be his people." This is variously referred to in theological tradition as the "election," the "vocation," and the "choosing" of Israel, all meaning roughly what the Catechism is here defining—the notion of Israel as God's people. The confusion stems from omitting the purpose phrase from the sentence—"to bring all the nations of the world to him."

If this phrase is left out, the "election" of Israel sounds like, has connotations of, arbitrary favoritism. It has thus contributed to the appalling history of anti-Semitism. The Bible speaks of God favoring certain people, but not the children of Israel. Their election has nothing to do with special status or favor, but is strictly a "task-oriented" election. They have a job to do, a service to render. Far from resentful, the rest of humanity should be grateful.

Therefore, *vocation* probably is the best word for the calling of Israel to be God's people, as it is referred to in Eucharistic Prayer B on page 368 of the Book of Common Prayer. Significantly, this is the oldest Eucharistic prayer ever included in an Anglican prayer book. *Vocation* in Scripture, and in Judeo-Christian tradition at its best, is never to be understood without purpose. God calls groups and individuals to do certain tasks. Usually, this involves hardship rather than worldly gratification. In the case of Israel, the task is global in scope.

These considerations raise an interesting perspective on mythology and history. The language of the preceding analysis is "mythological," but the phenomenon it describes—unlike that of the rebellion in the garden, for example—is supposed to take place in historical time, not mythic time. Both biblical and non-biblical ancient historical scholarship now tends to consider Abraham to be at least partially a historical figure, and to consider all scriptural story once Abraham appears on the scene in Genesis 12 to be potentially historical.

Fundamentalists naturally understand everything prior to Abraham's appearance as historical (or scientific or factual) as well, but they do not provide the only other serious interpretive option. On the contrary, a century ago the best scholars considered virtually the entire Old Testament, with but few exceptional passages, to be essentially fabulous—that is, to be fiction. The lists of kings they had to accept, since there is corroborating evidence, but the details of the narrative were rejected categorically.

Twentieth-century scholarship has retreated considerably from such skepticism. Recent archaeology has demonstrated that many details thought fanciful, such as the gigantic size of the stables of Solomon in Kings, are factual. The historical accuracy of the Old Testament has been reinforced at virtually every turn, lending special weight to the traditions, such as the election of Israel, handed down along with that history.

Yet that is precisely the way we must express Old Testament tradition—as "handed down along with" history. For God's action cannot be expressed as part of history itself, even though we believe it happens in a historical context. The reason is easy to see. History is always, potentially, corroborative. Material or literary or cultural evidence outside our religious tradition can "prove" any historical assertion—many now claim there is this sort of corroborative evidence for the flood in Genesis, for example. But God's self-expression is always by definition revelation, not history. Even if there were incontrovertible evidence of a universal deluge—which there is not—this would not establish that God had sent it, except in the sense that if God exists, God sends virtually everything.

On the other hand, it is essential for our tradition to express its historicity and to express it early. We believe that our myths express truth at a deep level, but we also believe that a great deal of the specific content of our tradition took place historically, not mythologically, that it is fact as well as truth. Indeed, very little in Scripture takes place once upon a time or in never-never land.

What response does God require from the chosen people?

To be faithful, to love justice, to do mercy, and to walk humbly with their God.

This a direct quote, almost complete, from Micah 6:8. It is often used as a summary of prophetic teaching, since it is set up as a summary in Scripture by the question, What does God require of his chosen?

The novelty is that the verse is being used as a catechetical answer. As stipulated at the beginning of our study, catechesis explains Scripture. It puts the mythological language into other words, usually more rationally oriented, less symbolic. Here, scriptural language is being used directly as part of the explanation rather than providing the material to be explained.

Why? Because the language is no longer that of mythology; nor is it the language of historical narration. This is prophecy, and the nature of prophecy is to clarify, not to mystify. There is neither mystery nor ambiguity in the biblical prophets, unlike the prophecies of the oracles in Greek tradition.[24] Micah's demand can be followed, rejected, or ignored. It does not require interpretation. Therefore, catechetical explanation in other words would be redundant.

Now this section, we claim, is the second half of the covenant—the part of the agreement to which the people consent. It is contained in the prophet Micah, but is paralleled in several other places. The "promise," by contrast, appears in words spoken to Abraham in the second quarter of the book of Genesis. Therefore, the answer to the question, Where is the covenant to be found? is, "in the books which we call the Old Testament." *We* for the first time in the Catechism means "we Christians"; Jews call these books "the Bible."

The operative phrase in the above discussion is "contained in." Often we speak of the Old Testament and Old Covenant as if they were interchangeable. They are, if we understand "Old Testament" *not* to mean the collection of books. We believe that the covenant, the testament, is contained in the books—but that it not to say it is coextensive with them. The Empire State Building can be found in the city of New York; and may serve as a symbol of the city, but it is not the same thing as New York. Our Catechism does not support the "verbally inerrant" theory of Scripture, according to which God is responsible for every word, and therefore every phrase is "inspired" or "infallible." Rather, we believe, as Martin Luther stated, that the Bible is like the manger at Bethlehem. It contains the Christ child, and it also contains straw. We are also free to understand the Bible as a toolbox. Its tools are meant to be helpful, but, in the wrong hands, a tool becomes a weapon. This has happened again and again in our checkered history, and to deny it makes it that much easier

---

24. Consider Croesus, who asked what would happen if he engaged the Persians in battle. He was told that a great kingdom would fall, took this as encouragement, attacked, and saw his own great kingdom defeated.

for thoughtful skeptics to dismiss us as wishful thinkers or downright scoundrels.

Past misuse of the Bible also, more positively, reminds us that there is a great deal more to the Bible than the covenant. The covenant is the centerpiece, but surrounding it are myth, history, poetry, wisdom, and miscellaneous items of interest. The approach to Scripture emerging in the Catechism recognizes key centers of focus which most clearly express God's will and nature. The next section, examining the Ten Commandments, depends on this idea.

Sin and Redemption

The Ten Commandments show us something about ourselves. They are, to use a medical metaphor, a diagnostic tool rather than a medicine. They show us our sinfulness, but they do not show us a way out of it or a cure for it. Christians who think that they observe the commandments deceive themselves. We break them every day. Our everyday sense of what the commandments ought to be—a guide for pragmatic living—is thus devastated. No guide that cannot be followed has value. Our catechetical explanation forces this awareness upon us, if the commandments in their prohibitive form do not.

That they "define" our relationship with God and our neighbors, however, suggests that they are nevertheless important and that they are binding upon us. Human cultures throughout the world have produced codes of behavior remarkably like the Ten Commandments. C. S. Lewis cataloged many of them in one of his most mature apologetic works, *The Abolition of Man*. Thomas Aquinas thought them so natural that, although God did reveal them, that revelation was not strictly necessary. Any intelligent person could also "reason them out" (*Summa Theologiae* Ia.19.11).

Given, then, a simple set of standards we feel compelled to obey, yet which we know ourselves unable to follow, we seem to be in an inherently frustrating situation. We seem again to be standing alongside one of Franz Kafka's antiheroes, being punished for transgressions we never had the option of keeping. Our existential situation begins to feel desperate and unfair; we are ostriches commanded to fly.

Clearly, something is wrong. Sin, our tradition tells us, is that something. We have already considered this concept as we cautiously answered the question of our alienation from God, but we studiously avoided the word *sin*. Now we examine it, but with a similar caution, and for similar reasons.

The relationship between sin and the commandments suggests that sin is not a matter of breaking the commandments. Sin is what makes us unable to keep them. If we try, for example, to "rejoice in other people's gifts and graces," and found ourselves unable to do this—even when willing—the command has helped us to "see more clearly our sin." Sin in this light begins to look like injury or illness, as a broken leg can prevent a woman from walking her dog though she had every "good" intention of doing so.

Reflection on ordinary language shows us that when we do break a commandment—when we lie—we say, "That is a sin," or "I have sinned." We might on reflection agree that it was sin that hindered us, but we insist that our action was also a sin. This conception makes sin look again like a matter of law. Following the law is acceptable but failing to follow it is sin. This line of thought reverts to the notion that the commandments as laws are solutions, not diagnostic tools.

Sin has characteristics of both realities. It is an illness and the breaking of laws. Like disease, it is within us, and like breaking laws, it involves external, objective principles and free will. We seem simultaneously to be invalids and lawbreakers, to be pitied and blamed. We are loath to part with either model, conflicting though they seem to be.

Christian tradition at its best tries to account for both aspects of the reality, to understand sin as part of our existential condition. Thus the Catechism defines it:

Q. What is sin?

A. Sin is the seeking of our own will instead of the will of God, thus distorting our relationship with God, with other people, and with all creation.

Sin is thus defined entirely in theological terms—in reference to God. This is legitimate, since the reality of God has already been treated at considerable length. It is important for us to note that our definition will not be satisfactory in naturalistic terms. It is based on the entire theology of creation sketched at the beginning of our study, wherein God, as author of the cosmos, has prerogatives, and wherein humanity, as the climax or centerpiece of that creation, enjoys privileges (and preeminence) within limitations.

An indispensable word in the definition is *will*. Thomas Aquinas made will the condition of sin: "Even when bodily desires are involved, sin is really committed through the will" (*Summa Theologiae*, Ia Iiae 83.1). Sin, as our tradition understands it, involves volition—wish and intent. It is not, as in classical tradition, a matter of *hamartia*, which meant "missing the mark" as in an archery contest. In Judeo-Christian theology, sin involves aiming at the wrong target—intentionally and with full awareness—for no other purpose than asserting the power to do so.

Sin involves a failure to recognize one of the supreme paradoxes of reality—that as created beings, we are most autonomous when we acknowledge our single point of dependence. In St. Augustine's words, "In God's service is our perfect freedom." It is perfectly reasonable that a created being should be interested in freedom, as Augustine explained. Hegel claimed that freedom is the key element in human consciousness and the value we desire most. Autonomy is one of the charisms God gives us to carry out our purpose in life. We could not be what we are without it.

But we "lose our liberty when our relationship with God is distorted." It is distorted when we seek our freedom absolutely. The paradox is that we cancel the very value we seek by failing to admit our limits, which in comparison with other creatures are minimal. As the poet John Donne wrote, "[E]xcept you enthrall me, never shall [I] be free; / Nor ever chaste, except you ravish me" ("Holy Sonnet").

Augustine himself offers in prose what may be the classic example of this principle, of freedom-seeking that is visible sin. His *Confessions*, his spiritual autobiography, does allude at various points to a dissolute life in the cities of the decadent Roman Empire, but his most bitter recriminations are surprisingly reserved for an incident from his youth, one most readers would at first glance dismiss as a boyish prank. Augustine and his friends, out for an afternoon of adolescent revelry, raided a neighbor's pear orchard. He tells us that they were not hungry and that the pears were not very good, or, as we would say, not "tempting." The neighbor had done them no spite. There was no ordinance to rebel against nor an audience of adolescent girls for whom to show off. Any of these elements would have softened the sin.

In other words, there was no natural catalyst for the behavior—no hunger or anger was involved. It seemed therefore to Augustine a pure act of the will and, therefore, on mature reflection, about the worst thing he had ever done, far worse than theater going (which in the Roman Empire was an arguably good deal more horrendous than in any other era), sexual liaisons, or the gluttony and revelry in which he subsequently engaged. Augustine almost presents the latter incidents as things over which he had no control, as though the incident with the pears caused the other behavior. It was almost as though his entire miserable career began with a single incident involving forbidden fruit.

Later Christian teaching agreed with Augustine and expressed in a simple diagram what he expressed in dramatic form. The "sin" involved with the pear theft would be labeled "pride," while the other matters he reveals about his early life involve lust, gluttony, envy, and so forth. These are the Seven Deadly Sins, a list which began to take shape in the early patristic period and by the later Middle Ages had taken its place alongside the commandments as the basis of Christian morality.[25]

Unlike the commandments, the seven sins are not specific transgressions but dispositions within the individual. Lust, for example, is not an action but the result of an action, or a description of a behavior; adultery is an action. The list indicates (among other things) an incipient awareness that sin has illness characteristics as well as legal characteristics. As Jesus suggested, it is one thing not to commit adultery and quite another to eliminate lust from the heart.

This is the first strength of the list of deadly sins. The second is its order, fixed very early and expressed in great monuments of

---

25. The history and origin of the traditional list may be found in Morton W. Bloomfield, *The Seven Deadly Sins*.

medieval art. The Gothic cathedrals expressed them in stone, Dante in poetic image, and Thomas Aquinas in philosophical language. The order is lust, gluttony, sloth, anger, greed, envy, and pride—a "bad to worst" order. Lust is least of the seven, because it is the only one that involves the well-being—albeit perversely perceived—of another human being. The list moves on to greater self-absorption. Envy, the second most heinous sin, involves reference to another being, but pride, the worst sin, is totally removed from others. It is the sin involved in Augustine's pear banditry—sin at its purest, the clearest example of "seeking our own will" when it gains nothing but the fact of having sought it.

Here a classic philosophical theory is implicitly rejected. We say that pride is the "worst" sin, and yet we realize that it does the least harm to others. Pure pride on the part of my neighbor, for example, cannot bother me nearly as much as his anger, stealing, lies, or gluttony. His pride, if it is pure pride, will be invisible. At least one school of moral thought would have concluded that that pride, being harmless, was the least of possible evils. In the eighteenth century, the same rationalist impulse we have already examined attempted to quantify and rationalize ethics through a philosophy called utilitarianism. According to this theory, any act should be valued for the amount of good it does for the number of people it affects or condemned for doing the most harm to the greatest number. The philosophy is a well-intentioned effort at making objective an area of experience fraught with subjectivity. One problem with it, however, as critics were soon to point out, is that it leaves the judgment of "amount" subjective. Should I sacrifice my life, if by donating my organs I shall save the lives of six other human beings? The immediate utilitarian answer would seem to be "yes," although few would agree. Perhaps the reluctance to agree lies in the question of how much pain the sacrifice of oneself would cause—perhaps seven times the pain of a natural death such as the six patients were facing? In that case, the answer would be "no." In any case, we have no means to measure.

In the case of Augustine's crime against the pear owner, the interpretation is clearer. The pain caused was minor, perhaps negligible. Perhaps the orchard owner never missed the pears. In that case, in a utilitarian scheme, the crime amounts to almost nothing, and certainly is not as "bad" as Augustine having lived with a woman for many years, which he assures us did cause his (saintly) mother plenty of pain.

Augustine judges the stealing harshly not for the amount of pain it causes, though, if his psychological analysis is right, it did "cause" much subsequent sin and misery. Rather, he judges it as the Catechism does—as distorting his relationship with God, with other people, and with all creation. His relationship with God is distorted since God knows what Augustine did, as are his relationships with the owner of the orchard and with pears. The act hurt Augustine, and whether it hurt anyone else, in the ordinary sense, is not the point. The philosopher who tried to answer the utilitarianism, Immanuel Kant, found himself falling back on Judeo-Christian tradition, calling for a categorical imperative as the basis for all ethical decision making, which he defined as the ability to universalize any action: could you wish this were a universal principle everyone had to follow? In other words, a philosophical version of the golden rule, not two steps away from our traditional examination of sin.

Q. What is redemption?

A. Redemption is the act of God which sets us free from the power of evil, sin, and death.

Our exploration of theology begins to turn, for the first time, in a specifically Christian direction. Not completely, for this question is easily asked within the context of the Old Covenant. But the answer anticipates the Christian solution to the problem of sin by the words "sets us free." As noted above, sin involves the desire for freedom, and, paradoxically, its loss. The created person has limits by definition and therefore his or her freedom is limited. The choice is not between absolute freedom and bondage to God, but between the relative freedom of God's service and being enthralled to sin. This is what Thomas Aquinas refers to when he defines sin as "any act contrary to right reason" (Ia Iiae 71.1). This definition was not introduced at first because it is so easily misleading, as though sin were like a mistake in mathematics or like the Greek idea of *hamartia*, meaning to miss the mark. Aquinas's definition means, rather, that humans miss the complexity of the choice in their desire for freedom, and that is the basis of their sin. The choice of absolute freedom leads not to freedom, but to its loss.

Loss of freedom implies thralldom. Mythically, this has been explained by reference to an extrabiblical tradition concerning Satan, the prince of evil angels. We will examine these explanations in some detail when we encounter the theological tradition of the atonement. For now we affirm instead the earliest Christian tradition, which understood humanity to be enslaved to "evil, sin, and death." The language here sounds Eucharistic. It is very close to the wording of Prayer B, which, as we have already seen, is the oldest of Eucharistic prayers. This prayer speaks of God "setting us free" from other powers, as opposed to the much later Eucharistic Prayer A, which speaks of Christ's "sacrifice." These powers make human life miserable. Existentially, this sounds reasonable, that creatures of limited power but unlimited imagination, self-conscious and painfully sensitive, would, given the choice, not choose evil, sin, or death. The materialist response is that these powers are natural, a permanent part of existence. The Christian attitude is that these powers are unnatural and temporary, the result of human perversity's having altered the natural system.

Interestingly, the Catechism here mixes metaphors. God redeems us, pays a debt for us, and yet the action is defined as setting us free, which suggests that we are not in debt but in prison. The mixture is due to alternate theories which, again, we will investigate when we examine the atonement.

The next question similarly echoes our Eucharistic Prayers. God "sent the prophets to call us back to himself, to show us our need for redemption, and to announce the coming of the Messiah." Prayers B, C, and D have three functions: to reveal God's message in such a way as to call us to return to God; to show us our need for redemption; and to prepare the way for the Messiah by focusing our consciousness more clearly upon him. That is an entire theology of prophecy in brief, and deserves closer examination.

First, the prophets "call us back." They do this by focusing God's will for us; that is, they clarify it, make our ethical imperatives more clear. In a sense, there is no such thing as a new morality in the prophets, nor in later Christian tradition. It is all there in the old law. But the prophets emphasize implications of that law that human frailty tends to blur. Thus the prophets seem constantly to refer to responsibility toward the helpless, the poor, the widowed, the orphan, and the oppressed, and to emphasize such moral behavior and such sweeping moral abstractions as justice over cultic behavior.

Second, and logically following, they "show us our need for redemption." In other words, they do what the commandments have been said to do already. In traditional theological language, they "convict us of sin." The prophets are thus extensions of the same revelation that is made in the ethical instruction in the Law, but they make it more dramatic and apply it more specifically. They constantly oppose religious complacency and thus cultivate a sense of dread, or holy terror, in the face of the expectation of the nearness of God (see Zephaniah 1:7).

Finally, they point to the coming Messiah. They "prepare the way," as John the Baptist is said to prepare the way in Christian tradition. In this function alone they fulfill the popular concept of the function of a prophet, which is "to predict the future." Almost never do biblical prophets predict the future. Occasionally they make specific threats concerning the future, but these are contingent upon certain patterns of behavior changing or not changing, which is different from prediction.

Only in the case of messianic prophecy can the prophets be said to predict what is coming, and in this case their message is complex and often ambiguous. On the one hand, the Messiah is to be a powerful and kingly figure, the heir of David and the champion against foreign oppression. On the other hand, he is to be meek, wretched, unattractive, and full of suffering. Yet again, he is to serve as a conduit for all nations to be brought to Yahweh—thus serving the purpose of Israel herself.

What these seemingly contradictory themes have in common is the advent of the Messiah. This figure is part of the future God has in store for Israel and for the world. How the contradictions will be resolved remains to be seen.

The questions on sin and redemption serve as a hinge between the second and third parts of our exploration, between the category "God the Father" and the category "God the Son." The Ten

Commandments, as the summary of ethical theism, sum up all our teachings about the Father. Our failure to keep the commandments—our failure, that is, to keep our half of the covenant—is the reason, as traditional theology has always understood it, for the second stage of our experience of God, the reason we need a New Covenant.

This section is therefore drawing to a close. We have been concerned throughout with the idea of God the Father, and we have examined that concept and its implications. We have at the same time explored the concept and content of the Old Covenant, since we understand that to be in some sense the vehicle for our particular understanding of God as Father. We have also, however, suggested that this doctrine is coterminous with the realm of natural theology. This is to put three concepts—God the Father, the Old Covenant, and natural theology—into close relationship. In summary, we can now refine that assumption and that relationship.

Natural theology expresses, as we have said, what we can know about God by employing our native faculties, such as reason and feeling. The traditional arguments for God's existence—cosmological, ethical, and so on—fall into this category. The doctrine of God as Creator, for most faith systems, also belongs in the delineation of natural theology. Anything beyond natural theology supposedly depends on specific revelation—roughly, what God revealed through the Christ-event.

Some theologians would claim that natural theology and the Old Covenant are congruent, that they cover the same ground. They would, in brief, add God's moral directives to the facts of God's existence and God's creatorship to form the content of natural theology. Immanuel Kant, for example, famous for trying to pinpoint the limitations of reason, also asserted that humanity has, in addition to reason, other native faculties such as emotion and conscience, which are also reliable as arbiters of reality and which reveal to any human being who uses them properly the fact and content of ethical monotheism. In other words, even without sacred Scripture, any rational human being can discover for him or herself that God exists, that God created the cosmos, and that God is concerned with correct human behavior. A great

deal of evidence actually supports this statement. How else to
explain, for example, the family resemblances among moral systems around the world and throughout recorded history?

At the opposite extreme we find those who deny that natural
reason or any other unaided faculty can discover anything about
God. The modern Protestant theologian Karl Barth, whom we
have already discussed in his apophatic aspect, is the most recent
example. Barth would see himself as merely the last in a long list
of theologians throughout history, including Augustine, Luther,
and St. Paul, who distrusted human faculties. This is what Barth
understood the classic notion of salvation by faith alone, *sola fide*,
to imply. Most if not all students of these earlier thinkers would
agree that Barth is telling us here a great deal about Barth and less
about Augustine, Luther, and Paul. What we know about God,
says Barth, we know because God has told us—directly, through
the content of revelation. If our reason later happens to agree, as
the later Barth came to put it, well and good, but revelation comes
first. There is no such thing as a priori knowledge of God, nothing
of the sort of knowledge, for example, that modern philosophers
beginning with Descartes sought to find.[26] Curiously, the serious
agnostic usually bases agnosticism on the same idea. The agnostic
states that there may indeed be a divinity, but if such a being exists
it is so far beyond human mental powers as to be inaccessible.

Barth hastens to add that God has revealed God's nature
through the reliable means of the Judeo-Christian revelation,
especially the Christian revelation. But Barth was categorically
opposed to the very idea of natural theology. To Barth it violated
notions of God's otherness and human limitation even to enter-
tain the possibility. To the logical objection of the atheist—if that
is true, how do we know, given humans' limited and tainted mental apparatus, that the revelation itself is valid?—Barth, unsur-
prisingly, offers no answer.

The philosophical atheist trusts reason, though usually without
establishing the trust of reason as a premise, then says that reason

---

26. Descartes insists that the existence of God is the second certainty
available to him, second only to the certainty of his own existence, established by his thought.

tells us that God does not exist. The atheist states that there is too much suffering in the world to allow for a God who is both powerful and moral, for example—a precept and a challenge Christians should be willing to take seriously, and which is taken seriously throughout this book. Any question of special revelation the atheist refutes as simple fantasy, whether as wish fulfillment and projection (Freud's position), or as oppressive tool (Marx). In other words, the atheist denies the possibility of any theology—natural or revealed.

Most theologians operate somewhere between the extremes of Kant and Barth. Most would agree with Kant's ethical argument for God's existence, but would add that the Old Covenant revelation made this clear and definite in an unparalleled way. Many would add, moreover, that the Christian revelation is consistent with the nature of God revealed through much of the Old Covenant. That God is compassionate, even suffering, is, as Abraham Heschel has asserted, strongly represented in Old Testament tradition—in the prophets especially but, also, if we look carefully, in the Torah as well. Christian theologians have been delighted to agree, and to accept the prophets as preparatory to the New Covenant.

God's Fatherhood remains somewhat problematic, to put it gently. We have tried to demythologize or, to use a popular literary-philosophical term, to *deconstruct* the symbol. This means that we will appreciate Fatherhood as a symbol and make sure we do not mistake it for something else. To a lesser extent, we have tried to do the same with several other traditional terms and symbols, such as *almighty* and *seen and unseen*. We have at least tried to "translate" these terms to make them accessible to the contemporary seeker or believer. Despite what many traditionalists may assert, these are not simple, commonsense notions, but complex, culturally weighted terms. I hope we have made that statement almost axiomatic. We will return to this method when we approach the idea of Jesus as Son. For now, we have tried to note the problem of definition while at the same time doing justice to the tradition and suggesting ways the symbol may be helpful, even to those who at first might find it a barrier, as many now do.

Less controversial should be the dynamic of our next move. The reality of sin—or whatever demythologized term might be substituted—is lost on virtually no one, whether Kantian or Barthian, agnostic or traditionalist, atheist or theologian, you or me. The eighteenth-century concept of this as the "best of all possible worlds," and held at the time by the best minds alive, seems almost repugnant to our minds.[27] Though we may question his attitude toward natural theology, we can appreciate Barth's clarity on this point. He reaffirmed the Pauline doctrine of grace, of God's gift and remedy.

When there is poverty, gifts are called for. When there is sickness, a remedy is needed. That, in short, is our next subject.

27. To do justice to the concept, however, we must understand that it did not represent a jejune and optimistic evaluation of this world, but began with an admission of its deeply troubled nature.

−5−

A Christology

Odor of blood when Christ was slain
Made all Platonic tolerance vain,
and vain all Doric discipline.

—WILLIAM BUTLER YEATS,
"TWO SONGS FROM A PLAY"

We turn to the subject traditionally called *Christology*—the "word about Christ." The name of the subject is shorthand for the doctrines and controversies which have swirled about his person from the earliest days of the Christian experience to the present. We thus leave the field of general monotheism and enter that of Christian revelation, where Christian claims are staked.

It is controversial territory. Even before the New Testament was "completed," or assembled, rival views of who and what Christ had been or was were being expressed. The New Testament never resolves the rival views, rather giving evidence for them all. The four Gospels exhibit examples of these differing viewpoints, interpretations, theories, and teachings at work.

To grasp fully differing interpretations of Christ may be difficult for contemporary Christians. Four documents as divergent as the Gospels can pose a challenge for anyone brought up in a Christian tradition, since Christian teaching tends to harmonize and reconcile the Gospels, smoothing over differences and playing down contradictions. To offset this tendency, try to imagine that you have never heard the gospel story—that you are a newcomer to the Christian faith. In that frame of mind, read through an entire Gospel. Make a page or two of notes about the story, including material such as the sequence of events, names, and geographical references. One full week later read a second Gospel, with your page of notes near at hand.

Like the earliest Christians, you may find yourself surprised and a little confused. These documents are but four of the bewilderingly divergent sources the first Christians employed for teaching. Only by the time of the third-century creeds was there anything like consensus on the question of a Christian center or orthodoxy. The Creed, in its central section, articulates that consensus position on what Christians believe to be the truth about Jesus. Our Catechism, in turn, attempts to explain that position, and a curious thing happens. The Catechism, normally expansive and discursive, suddenly contracts, and the longest part of the Creed becomes the shortest part of the Catechism. Why?

There are several reasons, but one reason is the cause of controversy. It is not that Jesus means different things to different people, and that a great deal of subjectivity is involved in Christology. These reasons would seem to demand more, not less, explanation. The main reason the catechetical section on Christology is abbreviated is that it expresses the irrational. Consider this: natural theology is, to most minds, very reasonable and, as its name suggests, natural, "familiar"; there is nothing puzzling or strange about it. Thus even those who reject theism as wishful thinking or self delusion find nothing baffling in its logic. Our traditional arguments for the existence of God, for example, can be appreciated even by the atheist who rejects them or the agnostic who suspends judgment, just as, roughly, he or she might appreciate the symmetry of a piece of religious music or a Romanesque cathedral.

Christology, in contrast to natural theology or theism, is utterly baffling to the outsider. As Paul expresses the concept the doctrine of Christ is a scandal to Jews and a stumbling block to Greeks—to anyone standing on the outside looking in. Christians need to take Paul's words seriously. It is hard for the morally minded atheist to admire Christianity. To Karl Marx, Christianity looks like a prop to perpetuate economic inequality. To Edward Gibbon, it looks like a historical virus that contributed to the downfall of the Roman Empire. We disagree, but we can appreciate these opinions. However lofty and useful Christian ethics in action may undoubtedly appear, Christian theology will always look, to the outsider, like the most vicious folly. Such an impression is vividly expressed in Yeats's lines at the beginning of this chapter. Christology makes no sense; it is paradoxical, thus compact.

At the same time, Christian theology has probably addressed Christology more than any other subject. The middle section of the Nicene Creed, which deals with Christology, is the longest. Unlike the Creed, the Catechism includes material on natural theology, reflecting our traditional understanding that much of what we know about God the Father falls into this category. This is information available through the senses and the use of reason. What we know about Jesus Christ, by contrast, is *revealed theology,* meaning that it includes what God has revealed of God's nature, beyond what we can discover on our own. Because it is God's most intentional and direct self-revelation, it conveys the most "information."

It is helpful to prepare for the next stage of the exploration with another apophatic reflection, which is in certain ways the opposite of what we have been doing to this point. Our method has been *kataphatic* or "affirmative." Thus, we have been constantly "asserting" and "affirming" theological realities. All systematic theology for the most part is kataphatic because it is, as observed earlier, discursive. It is an attempt to see how many reasonable assertions can be made concerning God.

Apophatic theology, as suggested in the second chapter, denies that much can be said. Anything we say about God, of whom we have no direct sensory experience, must be said by analogy. This is inadequate in every case. God is not great or good or loving in the analogical sense, since by those terms we can mean only what we have experienced, and God is infinitely beyond what we have experienced.

Since all language is analogous and each person witnesses only a limited fragment of the cosmos, the same criticism could be made for almost any assertion. The assertion has been made by Wittgenstein and by several other contemporary philosophers, who have said that not only theology, but every science, should be silenced.

Apophatic theology should stand as a constant reminder, however, of the limited nature of theology. The limitations extend not just to these pages, but to all theology. Theology is always analogous, always a matter of images, theories, working models, and temporary hypotheses—never a matter of certainty. Those who claim certainty for their faith, as in the statement, "I am certain Jesus is my Savior," are themselves speaking analogically whether they know it or not. What they are saying is: "I am convinced, emotionally, of this assertion."

In order to guard against any false sense of finality or completion, we have referred throughout to this project as an exploration. Although the topic we are about to examine—Christology—is two thousand years old, the subject is by nature so vast and complex that all theologians are in the exploratory stage.

We have also frequently used such words as *theory* and *model*. These are used intentionally and precisely. A theory is the best or one of the best explanations for a phenomenon that remains unexplained. It does not imply certainty or "prove" in the normal sense. In the twentieth century we have become accustomed to the theory of relativity, almost regarding it as a "scientific discovery," although it is not a discovery. The theory of gravity remains a theory, even though it was first articulated over two hundred years ago.

In this section we will encounter several theories concerning the doctrine of the atonement. These, like the scientific theories just mentioned, have seemed to account best for the phenomenon in question—our reconciliation with God through Christ—but none of them is "doctrine"; none of them has ever been "discovered." Similarly, the Church through the centuries approved and endorsed various theories concerning the Eucharistic words of Jesus and the nature of the sacrament of the Eucharist. None of these is doctrine. Anglicanism has generally held an agnostic position vis-à-vis such theories. It has never required adherence to any one of them.

A *model* is, similarly, a working tool. It bears resemblance to whatever it represents, yet is something different. Apologists from Justin Martyr to C. S. Lewis have understood theology to be analogous to a map. A map is a model that shares the elements of direction, proportionality, and arrangement with the landscape it represents. It is also unlike that landscape in that it is two-dimensional, portable, and legible. The balance of similarities and differences defines a good model.

This understanding of intellectual models is another way in which the experience of science in the past century may support rather than undermine Christianity. For example, most readers of this page will have a mental model of the solar system. This model will consist of spheres of various sizes—some with dull colors, some with horizontal rings—circling a larger, yellow sphere. When the model was first proposed, in the time of Nicolaus Copernicus and Johannes Kepler, it also seemed like a good depiction of the solar system, being what a hypothetical observer would see given the right observation point. We realize now that while the concept succeeds as a model, it fails miserably as a picture. The proportionate distances are hugely distorted, the actual orbits of the planets vary, and none of the shapes is circular or spherical, but more like ellipses. Further, twentieth-century physics has shown us that speed, shape, and time confuse the picture. All solar systems are immensely unstable, and the concept of a hypothetical observer makes no sense. Our model still works as a model, but the solar system does not "look like" this.

The model is based completely on earthbound realities, on the way we experience reality here and now, in our limited order. But a more faithful or accurate model would be unimaginable. An imperfect model is often the only possibility, which is why we were taught the Keplerian model of the solar system in childhood, even though science "knew better." The model we have is faithful and accurate as far as it goes and helps us understand the sequence of planets, the idea of orbit, and so on. As long as we realize that it is a model, and not a depiction, it serves its purpose. The model is partially true; or, better, it is useful, not true. It contributes to our appreciation of astronomical science.

The same principle obtains if we wish to appreciate theological science.[1] For example, we have already encountered one extremely important model for theology—the Fatherhood of God. God is not really a father. Judeo-Christian thought, as we have seen, is most careful to distinguish God from any such concept, in contradistinction to religions that understood God as a

---

1. Here I use the term *science* deliberately, as explained in the preface.

real father. Yet the model, by contrast, is eminently useful in revealing the depth and breadth of God's relationship to creation.

We are about to encounter a second great theological model, divine Sonship—for which the same reasoning will apply. Jesus is not in any biological sense the son of God. When we assert that he is, we must immediately qualify our assertion with an explanation that changes the sense of language. He is God's Son in a sense that is unique, which is unlike any other Sonship we have known.

It is simpler to explain the Sonship as a model that points and corresponds to a reality better than anything else we have discovered or been given. But it is not the reality.[2] The Sonship is no more the theological reality than our personal model of the solar system is the astronomical reality. It is "true" at a few limited points, but is hugely distorted and deceptive at others. This is not to demean the model, but to assert again that it is a model of theological reality—not a depiction. A depiction would, for our limited intelligence, probably be impossible.

All this is not the equivalent of saying "Jesus Christ is not the Son of God." It is rather to remember the strange confluence of Wittgenstein and the mystics, both of whom exhibit a sensitivity to the limits of language, which has often been lacking in traditional Christianity, which has often taken the truth of creedal assertions to be on the same order as assertions about worldly realities. Jesus is God's Son. If that sentence is understood in any ordinary, declarative sense, it is not so much false as nonsense. But understood analogically, it points to truth; symbolically, it expresses truth. All this reminds us that when we make this assertion, theology is spoken.

There is one way in which Jesus may be said unequivocally and without qualification to be the Son of God—not analogically

---

2. It is possible to assert that Christ is truly the son of God without changing the definition of the word son, and to do the same with God as "father," by taking a Platonic position that understands their sonship and fatherhood as ideal, as the "forms" of which human relationships of this nature are imperfect copies. I know of no other way, philosophically, of asserting that God is "really" or "literally" or "actually" or "truly" a father.

or symbolically, but literally, in the way Alexander was Philip's son. If human "sonship" is in reality a reflection or imitation of a perfect idea of Sonship in God's mind; if Jesus' son-relationship is the perfect pattern which all other son-relationships somehow copy; if Alexander's relationship to Philip is an imperfect "representation" of the God-Jesus archetype; then, and only then, Jesus is God's Son, without qualification. The problem with this view is that these concepts are borrowed from the dialogues of Plato. This approach assumes not only the truth of Christianity, but also the truth of Plato's worldview, of Plato's ontology. Many thoughtful Christians, such as St. Augustine, Origen, John Scotus, and John Donne, have believed in this approach. But many, such as Aquinas and almost all moderns, reject it. Platonism remains an option but never a requirement for Christian thinking.

The catechetical assertion that "Jesus is the only Son of God"—the capital letters indicate, as do quotation marks, a specialized use of any term—"means" that Jesus is the only perfect image of the Father, and shows us the nature of God. We deal here with what the New Testament scholar Oscar Cullmann called the "offense" of Christianity—its sheer particularity. Christianity claims that, from the point of view of history, a particular human being, of a certain gender and race, is the "midpoint of history." How can we deal with this "offense," which is offensive especially to the enlarged vision of world and time that the twentieth century has bequeathed to us? The best way to address the assertion is to imagine that we know nothing about "Christ" except that we have heard that he is "the only Son of God," and we want to know what this statement means. We do not know whether he is God, human, an alien species, or a fish. We know nothing but this assertion, and we hear the explanation that follows. What, honestly and logically, can we make of it?

First, we know that a human child often resembles the parent. Further, the child often reveals the nature of the parent, in that the character of the latter will in some sense be manifested in the former. The gender of the child is unimportant, in that daughters resemble the parents as sons do. Either gender can reflect the character of mothers or fathers. This much is intelligible: Jesus is the son of God in that Jesus shows us something abut God, and in that he resembles God, though not in a physical sense. We must next examine what we know about Jesus mentally and spiritually.

The word *image* leads us more deeply into this issue. The first affirmation in the Catechism read, "Humans are made in the image of God." It is taken, as noted, from the mythological language of Genesis 1, and is one of those rare instances in which the Catechism borrows directly from Scripture for its explanation. In this section of the Catechism we are told that Jesus is the "perfect" image of God. The two assertions establish a parallel relationship between Jesus and the rest of us. He is perfectly something we are imperfectly.

If we are God's image, and Christ is a perfect image of God, then Christ is the perfect manifestation of us. Christ is the perfect human being. No claim about his divinity has been made, since we, too, are called images of God. We deal here with a theory that Paul first mentioned in his first letter to the Corinthians and that was developed at length by the second-century theologian Irenaeus. The theory is called *recapitulation*, according to which Christ is the new Adam and the new representative human being—a new stage in evolution.

The second part of the assertion, that Jesus "shows us God's nature," also echoes the first question in the Catechism. Jesus is a being[3] who shares an image with us, but who seems to have an entirely different nature. Yet Jesus only seems to be different, for, as we shall see, he also shares our nature.

What is the nature of God revealed in Jesus? Notice as usual the careful wording. The question is not, What is the nature of God in general? for we have just explored that topic at length. What, instead, does Jesus specifically reveal about God? What do we know about God because of Jesus that we might otherwise not know?

---

3. We cannot call Jesus a person, or anything so technical. It is clear only at this point that Jesus exists—which is all a "being" is. It is the least specific noun in philosophy.

"God is love." While the heavens show the glory of God and the Old Covenant shows us God's authority and creativity, Jesus shows us God's love. More strongly, he shows us that God is love.

The word *is* sets up an equation and is far more comprehensive than has or does. Sometimes, however, this equation is an implicit metaphor, as in "God is a mighty warrior." "God is love" is a more challenging assertion, having greater force than stating that God is a king or father, because unlike these truths, it is nonliteral and nonmetaphorical. It is a straightforward, unequivocal assertion.

As we have already seen, the word *love* is multifaceted. We use it to cover an irregularly shaped spectrum of feelings and relationships, involving various attractions and duties. It is like our word *ocean*, for which South Sea island peoples have dozens of words. Where we see a single substance, undifferentiated, they see different substances, because they must live with the sea in its various conditions. They must know when it is navigable and how; they must understand it. Not to be able to do so, for a Maori, would be life-threatening.

For most speakers of English, although we use the word *love* automatically and without reflection in a number of ways, the word by itself—as in, "What is the meaning of love?"—refers to the emotion felt between mature humans, involving sexual attraction but also several other emotional components. If one were to canvass twelve people, asking them, without providing context for the question, what the word *love* means, at least two-thirds will answer in words that refer to sexual attraction. What do you expect to find if you see a book labeled "Love Poetry"? What message will you convey to a nonrelated adult if you say, "I love you"?

Psychology and aesthetics, as well as philosophy, have adduced a number of reasons for this predominant sense of *love*. Because love has to do with the survival of the species, leading as it does to reproduction and stable families, it is a powerful instinctive force. Freud reminds us of that. On the other hand, Western literary history suggests that it has been emphasized in our culture far out of proportion to its necessary place, exalted to such an extent that that we are far more sensitive to the romantic meaning of love than other cultures. Medieval studies has found this sensitivity in what it calls "courtly love."[4] This type of love, when qualified at all, is labeled "romantic" love.[5]

This romantic sense is not what we mean when we say that God is love. Use of the word *love* is not a metaphorical application as in the case of "God the Father." *Love,* in the everyday sense, and *love,* in the Catechism, are two separate and easily distinguishable things. In one key aspect, they are opposites.

The Greek language allowed for this differentiation with two different words: *eros* and *agape.* The Swedish Reformed theologian Anders Nygren said that the two words have "nothing to do with one another." This statement contradicts our analogical principle, but it underscores the vivid differentiation between the two concepts.[6] The first word, *eros,* has been devalued in our language as a reference to the erotic, which refers to sexual attraction pure and simple. But *eros* involved more than that, as *love* in the ordinary sense means more than sexual attraction. *Agape* is a noun practically coined by the early Christians from a minor Greek verb. They used the word to refer to the phenomenon they were experiencing as the love of God, or Christian love. The word in this sense referred to something otherwise indefinable, but involving a powerful positive emotion concerned with the well-being of another—a self-denying, other-regarding love. In this respect, *agape* is the opposite of *eros,* which though it seeks the well-being of the other is always, when fulfilled, deeply pleasurable.

---

4. Courtly love has in recent decades been seriously challenged by medievalists, leading many to write it off as a modern academic fiction. If this criticism is valid, and I believe it has a great deal of merit, that would mean that courtly love is a product of more modern erotic obsession, and thus lead us to the same conclusions about the phenomenon we are discussing.

5. A complex reference, having to do with the popularity of the subject in "romance" literature, originally referring to literature in the Middle Ages traceable to Roman origins. The reference also relates to its popularity as subject matter during the Romantic movement in literature of the nineteenth century.

6. Nygren's seminal study, *Eros and Agape,* should be consulted by anyone interested in this fascinating subject. Nygren tends to make agape the central Christian revelation, which I view as a serious distortion, but his insights into the entire question are indispensable.

The expression of agape, by contrast, can be deeply painful. All this may make agape sound remote and heroic, or otherworldly. Yet there are examples at hand. The parent who attends to a sick child in the middle of the night is an everyday example of agape at work. The parent does not "want" to get out of bed, but agape, self-denying love, alone impels the action. The deed is both prosaic and heroic, but is nonetheless agape.[7] The child, in trying to please the parent, is beginning to practice agape. In an erotic relationship, agape subtly moves in as the infatuation of eros dwindles and concern for the other as human being, as loving subject, replaces or joins itself to regard for the other as erotic object.

There are other levels or types of love, but, as Nygren argues in his *Eros and Agape*, these are the two supremely powerful manifestations of love. It is with agape that we are concerned when we claim that this is what God "is," and what Jesus "shows." Helpful at this point is to recall the "demythologizing" aspect of the Old Testament creation myths. In other accounts of creation, a great deal of eros was involved, but the Genesis account makes possible a loving God without erotic love. The Greek myths never separated the two. The father figure among the gods, Zeus, truly loves humankind, but he loves attractive females best, and goes to ingenious, grotesque, and comic lengths to gratify these erotic feelings. Conditioned by Judeo-Christian theology, we may find these myths startling, but they are not frivolous. Theologically speaking, they anticipate, in their very different way, the God who is Love whom we worship.

Here the strange and special logic of Christian theology begins to operate. Let us say that God is infinite, omniscient, omnipresent, and omnipotent. An infinite Being must be infinitely capable and inexhaustible. Therefore, there can be no meaningful "self-giving" for such a Being. There can be no loss when giving of infinity.

---

7. Some psychological theories would explain this action as instinctual. If this is true, then agape is built into the instinctual system. In no other instinct is self-preservation so effectively canceled.

Jesus, however, is finite. Soon we shall discuss the other implications of that finitude, but the first and most significant is that if
he gives of himself, he loses, as do we. Any act of self-donation or
self-denial must involve loss for it to be real. Jesus is capable of
loss in a way that God the Father, or, more accurately, the God of
natural theology, is not.

We can hear the words "God is love" and give assent to them,
but what do they mean? Had we said, "God is red," we could picture that redness. Had we said, "God is angry," we could grasp
that anger. But to say, "God is love," while it may sound "right"
because of our conditioning within the tradition, means little,
until we "observe" God in Christ.

What about Christ shows us this love? One thing, and one
thing only: his death. Jesus' life, as the four Gospels portray that
life, is not especially devoted to self-giving. It is a strikingly
unusual life, replete with challenge and revealing a character of
marked authority. Jesus engages in charitable actions and a number of courageous ones. We all know, however, if we are honest,
of lives that witnessed more to selfless love of others.

It could be argued that, while Jesus' life was not preeminently a
life of self-donation, it nonetheless served that purpose in that
everything he did, since he was perfect humanity, was self-denying.
But this begs christological questions. From the point of view of
theology, Jesus' self-denial is in fact true, but making the statement
assumes what we are working toward. We are now examining how
Jesus reveals God's love, and if his life is not one of self-sacrifice,
however replete with love it may be, it does not reveal love. The
Creed reflects this reasoning by saying next to nothing about Jesus'
life. Rather the Creed makes an affirmation about his birth, followed by several about his suffering and death.

That death, portrayed from the outset as a death understood
to have occurred on behalf of others, is the supreme act of
agape, the ultimate expression of love. That death also is the
single fact of Jesus' existence upon which all four Gospels
agree, down to the details. The oral tradition having transmitted
the facts about Jesus' death, the Gospels in turn came to be
about Jesus' death. It has been said accurately that the Gospels

are passion narratives, accounts of Jesus' last days, with prefaces added.

It is only when they come to the passion story that all four Gospels become synoptic. New Testament scholarship beginning in the seventeenth century, with the first application of secular literary techniques, has always made much of comparisons among the Gospels. Modern scholarship has taught us to regard the first three Gospels as the synoptics, the fourth as the unique or odd volume. When considering the narrative from birth to Jesus' entry into Jerusalem, that classification seems undeniable. But were there only the four accounts of the passion stories, it is doubtful that such a classification would have been suggested.

When reading the Gospel accounts of Jesus' death, ask the following "factual" questions: What was the nature of Jesus' betrayal? When did this take place? Who were the agents who effected his destruction? What was the reaction of the key disciples? Where did these things take place? What was the time frame? How long did Jesus take to die? At what time did he die? Compare the number of discrepancies with the number of consistencies. There will be points of disagreement, but they will be minor. On the major questions, the four accounts agree. Now try the same procedure for stories of the birth of Jesus. What does Mark have to say about Jesus' nativity? What does Matthew say about the census under Caesar Augustus? Where, according to John, was Jesus born? When, according to Luke, did the wise men arrive?

Those who are familiar with the Gospels already will realize that these questions have no answers, since there are no accounts of Jesus' nativity in Mark and John, and since Matthew and Luke offer stories almost impossible to harmonize and synchronize. We could perform the same experiment with stories of miraculous healings, teachings, the careers of the disciples. The result in every case would be a bewildering set of discrepancies. It is only when the narrative arrives at Jerusalem, at the beginning of the end, that, suddenly, the four Gospels begin to agree.

That is because at this point they examine the most important aspect of the story. We saw in the earlier example of agape—the parent getting up to care for the sick child—a sample of the nature of self-giving love. A little reflection, however, will suggest the imperfect nature of our example. For one thing, the parent knows that this action benefits him or her as well. The consequences of failing to act will be nearly as catastrophic for the parent as the child. The parent's web of human support will endorse the loving act or condemn the alternative, while the conscience will torture a failure to act. The act is essentially agapic, but by no means purely so.

The opposite is true of Jesus' death in the Gospels. There are no self-interested motives. His cause seems lost. His followers have deserted. His journey to the cross does not follow human instinct, nor does it make historical sense. Jesus' death is unlike many heroic deaths, which have the potential to inspire others. The cross represents total humiliation and shame. He does not go down defending a doomed position or to protect the lives of comrades, as many "Christ figures" in subsequent tales seem to do. In contrast to the death of Socrates, Jesus' death lacks intellectual consistency, asserted in the *Crito*.

It is difficult for us, conditioned by theological hindsight, to see Jesus' death in this way, but the Gospels make it clear that this is how Jesus' death should be seen. Did Jesus' death seem as meaningless to Jesus? Did he believe all was lost? Or did he, with divine insight, foresee his triumph? Luke 23:43 would suggest that he did, but the rest of the tradition, especially the account in Mark, suggests the opposite. Jesus abandoned omnipresence in order to be incarnate. The Gospels make it clear that he also abandoned omnipotence, for his powers are limited. It is a simple step from these considerations to reflect that he may have abandoned omniscience as well, and that, approaching Cavalry, he had no hint of the future. All he must know is that he is required to die for others—the meaning of which is also uncertain—if the death is to be perfect.

There can be only two possible explanations for Jesus' actions. Either he has entirely lost his mind and will, or he is acting solely out of agape.

This act of agape is the first great theological assertion of the Christian faith. As we have just seen, it also raises the first great paradox of the Christian faith—the Incarnation. This doctrine asserts that in Christ, God was "made" human, or made God's self human. The awkwardness of the words suggests the difficulty of the concept. Christ is, we assert, simultaneously human and divine. This is expressed by saying that Christ is the "divine Son," that Christ "received" our human nature. He is "Lord" and "brother" to us.

From the beginning, benign, well-meaning Christians have tried to solve this paradox by making it sound more reasonable. Such persons came to be called heretics, a word which has gathered connotations, some of which are, in this instance, extremely misleading. In past centuries, the word connoted an almost diabolical, willful participation in a malevolent, twisted Christianity, which was not true of the original heretics. Today it suggests a bold nonconformity, a spiritual and intellectual daring which the Church, in stodgy, threatened conformity, forbids and persecutes. Such Romantic fiction is not valid for the early christological heretics. If anything, the first heresies known to the Church were more "conformist" in that they tried to conform the faith to common sense or to reason. The Church could have been construed as the nonconformist reality, insistent upon the paradoxical nature of her truth, no matter how difficult or shocking.

One early tendency so accorded with common sense that many Christians at one point or another have been attracted to it. This notion understood Christ as a divine person who only appeared to have taken on human mortality and flesh, and thus it is called *Docetism*, from the Greek word meaning "to appear." It solves the paradox by denying the human side of the formula. It preserves the glory of the Transfiguration, but destroys the tableau at Bethlehem. We find the concept substantially developed at least as early as the second century, and we find Christian teachers almost from the outset at pains to refute it.

Even the Gospel tradition refutes this teaching. According to some scholarly interpretations, the birth and infancy narratives in the third Gospel are themselves refutations of Docetism. In the prologue to the Fourth Gospel, Docetism is more systematically challenged. In symbolic language John affirms both the eternal existence of the divine Word and his incarnate life. The divine Christ is portrayed as a Euclidean line, infinite in two directions, while the human Jesus is compared to a half-line, with a specific starting point but infinite in one direction.

The opposite tendency to Docetism involves understanding Jesus as a genuinely great human being, perhaps as the greatest human being who ever lived, but as a creature nonetheless. This tendency is most commonly called *Arianism*, after the ingenious third-century priest Arius who offered this platonically shaded view of Christian reality. Again, the Fourth Gospel counters this view with the assertion that the flesh-and-blood character many knew in person as a human teacher and friend was simultaneously the Divine Word, who had existed from before time, who was "with God" and who "was God."

Either alternative is more congenial to ordinary reason than the Christian assertion that Jesus was both man and God. The power of these rationalizations—to use the exact word—was and remains great. Many people will, as a moment's reflection suggests, be willing to accept Jesus in the Arian sense. How often have you heard someone assert, "I see Jesus as a great prophet, but not as 'God's Son' or anything as mystical as that"?

The Creed is careful to affirm both terms in the clearest language. Jesus Christ

1. is True God from true God; and

2. was made Man.

The Catechism is deliberately open-ended in its wording: "By God's own act, the divine Son received our human nature from the Virgin Mary, his mother." Exactly how this miracle occurred is not important theologically. In other words, the deeper miracle is not the Virgin Birth, but the Incarnation, the Word made flesh.

To paraphrase Paul, this concept, like the crucifixion, is problematic for both Jew and Gentile. Jews were (and are) conditioned by Torah to the doctrine of the supreme transcendence, the utter Otherness, of God, the attribute we stressed in the previous chapter. For such a God to take on human flesh is shocking. Similarly, Greek philosophy had moved painfully and slowly toward an intellectual apprehension of a nonmaterial, refined concept of a Creator-Deity. The Christian idea must have seemed to anyone conversant with this tradition to be a mental slip toward the anthropomorphism of the myths. Becoming incarnate was the sort of thing Zeus would do, not the creator of the *Timaeus*. Greek thought had advanced a great distance in the direction of harmony, balance, rationalism, and "Platonic tolerance." Christianity proclaimed a God who entered the human arena all bloody, and departed the same way.

Yet this was, and remains, the Christian claim. The teaching also remains difficult. No serious Christian thinker maintains that it "makes sense," since it does not. Understanding incarnation is a matter, as the Scholastic philosopher-theologians insisted, of revelation, and therefore must be accepted by faith, or rejected. It is at this point that we encounter one of the unexpected examples of support from contemporary science. It can be argued that we in the postmodern era find paradox more compatible, more intellectually acceptable, with our worldview than our immediate forebears. Modern science, resting on achievement which culminated in the work of Isaac Newton, thought of paradox as something to resolve; we do not. Small-particle physics, for example, has taught the principle of indeterminacy. Relativity has given us the profoundly counterintuitive model of curved space-time. Even for those who have penetrated the mathematics, these ideas involve a leap of faith. Like the Incarnation, they are paradoxical and unreasonable by nature. Yet also like the Incarnation, they profess to reveal deep reality.

Modern art and literature, similarly, may have conditioned us to accept absurdity and paradox as signposts on the road to truth, rather than as warning signals on the path to falsehood. We have given the phrases "too neat" or "overly rational" meanings which the Romantics might never have suspected. In short, we may be able again to appreciate the assertion of the second-century theologian Tertullian, *Credo quia absurdum est,* "I believe because it is absurd." The Incarnation seems less likely to be explained away as pious fantasy or wishful thinking. Rather, it seems more like the models of reality the best minds in secular culture have been offering for over a century.

On the other hand, once the initial paradox of the Incarnation is accepted, its implications and ramifications are not at all unreasonable—another point often made by the Scholastics. Once we accept the Incarnation as given, we can explore its effects more or less rationally. We may discover, moreover, that it does seem to account for things and to solve problems insoluble in any other way—exactly what happened in physics when Einstein's bizarre model was tested.

Why did the Incarnation occur? As the Creed asks, "Why did he take our human nature?" Because in this way, the Creed answers, "human beings might be adopted as children of God, and made heirs of God's kingdom." Again, a substantial history of thought and controversy lies behind this catechetical answer.

Consider that the Catechism in the 1928 Book of Common Prayer covers Christology in a single response: "I believe . . . in God the Son, who hath redeemed me, and all mankind." The current Catechism expands this statement. As we have sketched the Christology of the current Catechism, it begins with the nature of Christ. It continues by considering redemption, the single subject of the sentence quoted from the 1928 Catechism. The first emphasis with regard to redemption—that the divine Son became human to effect adoption as God's children— appears in the catechetical answer Note carefully that this redemption is not the purpose of Jesus' death, but of the Incarnation. This aspect demands careful explication.

By naming God "Father" in the first part of the Creed and in the second part of the Catechism, we imply that in some sense we are already God's "children," but only in the sense of our creatureliness, which we share with the rest of the cosmos. God is "Father," as we have seen, by virtue of his loving creativity. Nevertheless, we also affirmed, in our sketch of a Christian anthropology, that we are also made "in God's image"—which could suggest a special kinship relation, although not necessarily. Artists have painted self-portraits, for example, in "their image," which no one mistakes for their offspring.

Clearly, implied in our adoption is something different from the generic sense in which "we are all God's children." The ideas are simple enough, but the logic is complicated and needs some explanation. Our sin, as we have seen, has alienated us from God. Perhaps the simplest way to state this fact is that we have given up our birthright, like Esau in Genesis 25. We are too different from God to be adopted by God, given the reality of that alienation.

But if we could be adopted by God, what would that adoption logically involve? First, people are adopted by those who are not their parents. We are not God's children, if God can adopt us. In what sense is that statement valid and true? It is true, and valid, in the sense that Christ is God's child. He is divine, we are not. Beings "beget" beings of the same order of being as themselves: humans beget humans, hyenas beget hyenas, whales beget whales, and God begets God. Adoption follows the same rule, in that a human couple may legally adopt a human being but cannot adopt, however much they might want to, a hyena or whale. They could buy one, but purchase is not close to adoption. Were there another divine Being, God could adopt that Being, but God cannot adopt one of us. But by taking on our nature, being simultaneously God and homo sapiens, Christ becomes one of us and therefore an existential bridge between the two orders of being, human and divine. He thus makes our adoption possible.

For most contemporary Western Christians, this argument presents an unfamiliar way of expressing theological truth. Most such Christians are accustomed to the idea that God has redeemed us, not that God adopts us. That is another model, focused on Christ's sacrificial death, and is similarly valid. But it is not the only, nor necessarily the primary, christological reality.

The notion that we are adopted children of God is as ancient as the faith itself. Paul employs the idea in Romans 8: "[We have] received the Spirit of adoption, enabling us to cry out, 'Abba, Father!' The Spirit himself joins with our spirit to bear witness that we are children of God. And if we are children, then we are heirs . . . "(vv. 15b–17, NJB). It was a strong theme—or, better, thesis—in the early Church, as its presence in Eucharistic Prayer B testifies, wherein Christ "brings us to that heavenly country where . . . we may enter the everlasting heritage of [God's] sons and daughters" (Book of Common Prayer, 369). The ancient prayer echoes the thought of early theologians such as Irenaeus, whose recapitulation model we have already examined. The thesis of adoption is also strongly present in the second Postcommunion Prayer, in which we claim to have been made "heirs of [God's] eternal kingdom," having been "accepted" by God as living members of the Body of Christ.[8]

So the first model for what Christ accomplishes, prior to his death and resurrection, is our adoption. The second and the third models depend on the adoption.

Q. What is the great importance of Christ's suffering and death?

A. He made the offering which we could not make; in him we are freed from the power of sin (and reconciled to God).

The first phrase in this answer is the model most modern Western Christians will find familiar. It focuses not on the Incarnation, but on the atonement, the reconciliation of humanity with God, and it supposes that this involves an "offering."

That the offering is owed by humanity is clear. To whom it is owed, however, is not. Presumably the offering is owed to God, since it is to God that we are to be "reconciled." Further, since this involves "suffering and death," and "obedience," these must be the terms of the offering.

Since human beings are capable of suffering and death, presumably we are defective in obedience. Does this mean that Jesus' obedience is what God demands, and is what God accepts because it is more perfect than ours?

According to Irenaeus's recapitulation model of Incarnation, this obedience model would explain the atonement. The same line of thinking has been developed by contemporary German theologian Dorothee Sölle, whose *Christ the Representative* may be understood as a modern version of Irenaeus's view. Christ represents humanity, rather than "substituting" for us, and thus brings us "into the act" of redemption rather than leaving a helpless humanity out of the picture. This understanding has tremendous

---

8. This prayer is the older of the two alternatives in the current Book of Common Prayer. It is a version of the first Anglican Postcommunion prayer of 1549, which blended several medieval prayers into one theologically comprehensive concluding prayer. The other alternative is a modern composition, but also stresses ancient themes, like Eucharistic Prayer C.

value as a corrective to the passive-pathetic understanding of redemption which has tended to prevail in Western thought. But it is not the only way redemption can be understood, nor is it the primary understanding of our tradition.

Alongside the notion of our adoption and our inheritance of the kingdom of God, we find in the New Testament a theory according to which Jesus in dying paid the ultimate price, gave his life for humanity, and became a sacrificial offering. The idea of the worth of sacrifice, and the practice of sacrificing to the gods or to a god, seems as old as humanity and as universal. Every early and preliterate culture[9] shows evidence of the practice. Our everyday language betrays our (vestigial) sense that sacrifice is a deeply felt value. We speak of the "nobility" of sacrifice, of the "ultimate" sacrifice, of making sacrifices for one's friends, and so on, despite a post-Freudian popular culture which glorifies the individual. Sacrifice in and of itself seems a basic human aspiration.

Religious sacrifice in general has to do with propitiation of the gods. It is the opposite of magic, or the manipulation of supernatural forces, in that it involves human willingness to be supernaturally manipulated. The idea is that, for whatever reason, the gods become angry. Our lot will be miserable until we please them by offering something we are loath to part with.[10]

This is a strong but undefined concept. In Old Testament theology, by contrast, the theory and practice of sacrifice are highly developed, perhaps along more ethical lines than anytime in history. God is angry in the Old Testament with the transgressions of the human race specifically, and may be appeased by means of a rigid, rather logical, system of offerings. Although the cult of sacrifice in ancient Israel was complex, and developed in theological

---

9. "Preliterate" means not having developed literacy. It does not in my usage imply that any such culture eventually will, or should, develop literacy. The word has come into wide usage in anthropological discussion, replacing the much more pejorative term *primitive*, and this is my reason for using it.

10. Unless we trick them, as in the Greek myth of the origin of sacrifice, wherein the worst parts of the animal are wrapped in an attractive package, so that the humans can still enjoy a feast. The myth is a comic inversion of the idea of divine wisdom, and it supports our point. The myth is told, for example, by Ovid in his *Metamorphoses*.

sophistication over the centuries, it never lost its primitive sense of God's anger and the need for its appeasement.[11]

One central theme in the earliest Christian thought, then, is that Christ's death is a logical development of this sacrificial cult, or, rather, its culmination. Christ, in dying on the cross, achieved a permanent and complete sacrifice. Every former offering was partial. The human debt was never completely paid by the offerings of vegetables, birds, goats, and bulls. But Christ's offering was complete and need never be repeated. It was the termination of the practice of sacrifice, for any subsequent blood sacrifice would be redundant. The sheer weight of this concept inheres in our word *blessed*, which, though it translates a word from New Testament Greek better translated as "happy," relates through its original meaning, "to make sacred by the sprinkling of a blood sacrifice," to the word bloody.

This notion of sacrifice permeates the New Testament. Virtually every book, with the exception of James, presents or alludes to the idea in some form. The most completely developed statement appears in Hebrews, which scholars for years have believed to be a relatively late consideration of the relationship of Christianity to the Old Testament ritual cult. The summary in the previous paragraph essentially paraphrases the argument of Hebrews.

Certain questions, however, remain unanswered. Human alienation we can understand. But what is the debt owed to God? Why does Jesus' death suffice to pay the debt, while the deaths of many others in good causes do not? What, finally, is the relationship of Incarnation to this sacrificial death?

These questions were answered by St. Anselm, an archbishop of Canterbury in the eleventh century who also provided the defining statement of the ontological argument for the existence of God. His treatise *Cur Deus Homo*, or "Why the God-Man?" provides the classic definition of the sacrifice or propitiation theory. His definition is extremely important in the history of Christian

11. An excellent summary of the practice of sacrifice in ancient Israel, and of its theological development, may be found in Roland de Vaux, *Ancient Israel* (New York: McGraw-Hill, 1965), chaps. 10–14.

thought because it represents the dominant model of atonement in the Christian West. Although many now appreciate the significance of other theories, St. Anselm's work remains for most Christians the basic explanation of salvation.

According to Anselm's argument, the atonement is logical. It is an example of our contention that, once the paradoxical aspects of Christianity are accepted as axiomatic, other aspects can make rational sense. Anselm asserts that, by disobedience, humanity—Adam—becomes indebted to God. But since God's initial gifts to Adam were infinite, that debt is infinite, and therefore Adam, a finite creature, cannot pay it. Only a divine being can pay an infinite price. On the other hand, a son of Adam—a human being—must pay the price; otherwise, justice is not done.

The Incarnation, according to Anselm, solves the dilemma, and the crucifixion pays the debt. Christ is infinite as the divine Son of God. Christ is also human, being the flesh-and-blood son of Mary. All the Old Testament sacrifices, indeed all sacrifices made by humans for whatever reasons in whatever cult, become, for Anselm, anticipations of the sacrifice made by Christ, Platonic copies of the real act.

This is the model of the atonement that lies behind the catechetical words, "made the offering we could not make." We state the issue precisely when we say that Christ "paid the ultimate sacrifice."

The word *sacrifice* derives from two Latin words meaning "I make holy," *sacrum facio*. Christ's offering, besides "redeeming" humanity, also "makes humankind holy," or worthy to "stand before God," in the words of Eucharistic Prayer B. Thus "in him we are . . . reconciled to God." The Orthodox Church has traditionally emphasized this aspect of atonement (theosis). By Christ's death, we are sanctified, and our true or potential relationship of God is realized.

This is the dominant model of atonement in the West with Christian language from St. Anselm to the evangelical insistence that "Jesus died for your sins" to support it. This model seems to be the way most Christians envision Christ's saving act.

But it is not the only model. As already noted, the Incarnation itself provides a model of adoptionism. Orthodoxy has always emphasized this fact, along with the related doctrine of *theosis* just mentioned. A fourth possible understanding of the atonement is suggested by the words, "in him we are freed from the power of sin."

"On the third day," the Creed asserts, "he rose again." In a sense, this statement is the heart of Christian belief. As miracle, it is first and last, the greatest and most meaningful. The divine Sonship, the Incarnation, and the Virgin Mary, although chronologically prior, came later as matters of Christian belief. The first miracle Christians claimed as central to their faith was the resurrection, and it was to remain central. It is also the great stumbling block, the aspect of Christianity most difficult for others to accept. To this point, virtually everything in the Creed could be accepted by an intellectually generous skeptic, even the mention of the Virgin Mary.

Yet Christians boldly state that Jesus rose from the dead. It is not said that he "survived death" or that his soul or personality survived the material dissolution of his body. These notions would be acceptable to a majority of humanity. All preliterate peoples believe in the survival of the soul, as did Plato, who attempts to prove it logically in the *Phaedo*. The dichotomy between mortal body and immortal soul is a "natural" human model, found virtually everywhere and in all times.

By contrast, New Testament Christianity, following Old Testament anthropology, does not believe in the dichotomy and presents the human being as a "psychosomatic unity." In this move we again find a paradoxical, or at least an unexpected, parallel in contemporary philosophy. Gilbert Ryle, the British philosopher who took up the mantle of Bertrand Russell and was nearly as skeptical about religion, questioned the Platonic mind-body split as a serious delusion of language. According to Ryle in *The Concept of Mind*, René Descartes, arguably the founder of modern philosophy, failed at the crucial moment when, having reduced thought to its essentials, he preserved the notion of a spiritually divided creature, of humans as "composed" of two distinct orders, bodies and souls. Ryle called this the notion of the "ghost in the machine," and thought it denigrating to human dignity and a false picture of our experience, which is not dual, but unitary. He assumed without question, as far too many persons within and without seem to do, that the body-soul division was fundamental to Christianity. The idea, however, never was fundamental, and the "ghost in the machine" makes as little sense in the light of the New Testament accounts of Jesus' afterlife as it did to Ryle.

It is understandable that Ryle would miss the New Testament doctrine, (1) because it has been obscured even for many Christians by the Platonic division of body and soul; and (2) because no one believes in resurrection but Christians. The belief is paralleled or anticipated in the Egyptian myth of Osiris and the Greek myth of Demeter, but these were never connected with a historical person. Conversely, many cults assert that while their leader's body is destroyed, "his soul goes marching on." Christianity asserts the resurrection, the full, complete rising to life of Jesus, body and soul. The Greek word is *anastasis*, a wonderfully simple word picture meaning roughly "standing there all over again."

Other myths become important at this point. Bearing in mind our early definition of the word *myth* as a reality too great for normal explanation, told in narrative form, we assert that the resurrection of Jesus is indeed a myth. We also assert that it is a fact, verifiable by witnesses. Here is where our understanding of myth contrasts decisively with that of Rudolf Bultmann, who would agree that resurrection appearances are myths, but who then would dismiss them as fanciful, wishful imaginings, devoid of historical content and philosophical meaning. We insist on both dimensions of myth. We assert that in Jesus myth and history met, that in a sense the resurrection is a dream come true. Given that one of the most common human dreams is to survive death, that is what Christians believe happened to Jesus.

The postresurrection appearances of Jesus in the Gospels, and briefly in the opening of Acts, all refute the possibility that Jesus has become a ghost, or a resuscitated corpse. Though he is risen from the dead, there is nothing uncanny about him. He is himself and can, in exquisite detail, show the results of his former ordeal. He eats bread and cooks breakfast, and, as always, he teaches. He does not float and is not accompanied by supernatural beings or clothed in supernatural symbols. All mythological signals are missing.

The import of this understanding of the resurrection is colossal. As the Catechism explains, Jesus' rising is not merely a miracle demonstrating the power of God or the uniqueness of Jesus Christ. It is the culmination of the *Christus Victor* thesis that "by his resurrection, Jesus overcame death." Further, it is the means by which resurrection is extended to humanity, that by dying Jesus "opened for us the way to eternal life." This is the ultimate expression of the recapitulation theory. As Paul writes in First Corinthians, as in Adam all die, in Christ all are made alive.

This idea has been expressed in poetry by George Herbert, a seventeenth-century Anglican priest who anticipated many of the developments of twentieth-century poetry. Herbert expressed the idea when he begs Christ to "imp" his wing on his, a term referring to a practice in ancient falconry in which feathers from the wing of a stronger bird were "grafted" to improve the flight of a weaker bird.

We have said that once the miraculous or nonrational elements of theology are accepted, the other aspects can bear rational analysis. The next assertion—"he descended to the dead"—is an example. It answers the logical question, "If Jesus rose on the third day, what happened in between? What happened on Holy Saturday?" And it answers the question, "What happened to those who died before the Christian revelation?" Persons who object to modern theological language have objected to this statement in the Catechism, which replaces "he descended into Hell." But that was always a poor or misleading translation of the Greek in the Creed, which read, "he descended into *Hades*," which meant, simply, "the place of the dead," a vague, shadowy, and neutral concept. The Christian "Hell" had, in a sense, not been fully invented at the time of the Creed, but it was well on its way. The Creed never intended to put Christ there. Instead, like the later purgatory, Christians imagined a place where previously deceased persons, such as the Old Testament faithful, went before the appearance of Jesus. They believed that, before Easter Sunday, Jesus descended to them "and offered them also the benefits of redemption." The biblical warrant for this action is minimal. The deed is not described in the Gospels and rests rather on a minuscule and obscure passage in Paul. It became, however, a powerful conviction, as Christians were determined that the love of God must be as all-encompassing as possible, and Christ's victory as extensive as possible.

Another approach to this question begins by appreciating, with many modern philosophers, the relative and even fictional nature of time. The twentieth century challenged, then changed, our understanding of time; eventually, the change may affect popular consciousness, but that has just begun. As Bertrand Russell remarks in his useful book, *ABC of Relativity*, the new understanding of time is "for the imagination, the most difficult aspect" of contemporary science.[12] This is because we are used to thinking in terms of time as a constant, measurable, and standard reality. Time, we say, is "the same" anywhere and everywhere and that it affects all equally. Physics now says otherwise and has been saying otherwise for a hundred years. Time is relative to speed and position, so that someone traveling at a greater speed will experience time more slowly than an earthbound person, will age more slowly, and will see a different (earlier) time on his clock. In the model physics uses of "time neighborhoods," what makes sense, timewise, in one corner of the universe makes no sense in another.

Judeo-Christian theology has understood the relativity of time all along. The New Testament theology of Oscar Cullmann and Hans Conzelmann understood part of the challenge of Christianity to be its presentation of the idea that time might have a midpoint.[13] This is a curious notion for an entity supposed to be "infinite." But Scripture is replete with approaches to time that are counter to common sense. Biblical time has always been complex, as in Psalm 90, which asserts that a thousand years, when past, seem like a day to God. Theology has often posited a different time scale for numinous reality than for temporal reality.

---

12. B. Russell, *ABC of Relativity* (London: Allen and Unwin, 1958), p. 34.
13. Conzelmann's classic study of Luke was titled *Die Mitte der Zeit* (The Middle of Time).

A strong tradition in Christian theology holds that God is in reality beyond time, that time itself is in a sense fictional. Time in this sense exists as a handy device, but no more real than, say, a "meter" as a standard of measurement. This idea may seem to contradict common sense, but it is also what Stephen Hawking explains in A *Brief History of Time*. In a real sense, time does not exist, or at least does not exist "in nature." Time exists only as an artifact, a human invention.[14] This statement applies to any question, such as the nature of the afterlife, since, if God is beyond time, to enter eternity perhaps means to leave time and therefore to enter an eternal present. In the eternal present questions such as, "What happened to those who died before Christ?" lose their meaning. The person who dies leaves the "time neighborhood."[15]

Besides "making the offer we could not make," Christ's suffering and death also freed us "from the power of sin and death." This phrase sums up what is perhaps the defining model for the atonement, though, again, it may not be the most familiar to Western Christians. The liberating power is at least as ancient and as scripturally rooted as the more familiar understanding charted by Anselm. It is expressed virtually throughout the New Testament and also is strongly represented in worship life by Eucharistic Prayer D, the oldest complete Eucharistic prayer ever to appear in an Anglican prayer book.[16] That prayer dates from the fourth century, and is replete with the imagery of conquest and liberation: "[T]o fulfill your purpose he . . . destroyed death, and made the whole creation new." A similar concept is also directly reflected in the Prayers for Candidates at Baptism: "Deliver them, O Lord, from the power of sin and death."

For the first several centuries of Christian history, this was the dominant metaphor or model for Christ's atoning activity: victory

---

14. The philosopher Kant made this assertion in the late eighteenth century as a part of his deeply influential critique of metaphysics, but it was not until the twentieth century that this notion became a functional, practical part of the scientific model.

15. This concept also has practical implications for the question of cremation.

16. Prayer B is older but came to us in fragments. It is thus not complete, but was finished in the twentieth century by Frank Griswold.

over evil, rather than sacrificial propitiation (or redemption). The modern Lutheran theologian Gustav Aulen explains the history of the metaphor at length in *Christus Victor*. Christ for several hundred years was most frequently discussed in theology, and presented in art and poetry, as a warrior-hero, triumphing over the forces which enslave humankind. Almost never was he depicted as the pathetic victim and almost never as suffering on the cross.

It was not until Anselm, who worked out the theological logic for propitiation, that the image of Christ as sacrificial substitute became dominant. Whether Anselm effected this change, or merely reflected it, is impossible to say. What is clear is that, from the eleventh century, Christ was primarily understood in sacrificial terms and was more often depicted as suffering on the cross.

The hinge moment may be seen in a late Old English poem, the "Dream of the Rood." This work, which comes to us in its complete form from the tenth century, is remarkable in that it depicts Christ for the first time as triumphant warrior and as pathetic victim. It is virtually the last important work in which Christ appears in the former role.

The Christus Victor model provides Christ with an adversary. Christ in the redemption model is offered as a sacrifice to God. God the Father is the person propitiated in the Anselmian theory. In the Christus Victor model Satan serves as adversary, which is also the meaning of his name. Satan has imprisoned humanity and holds Adam as prisoner of war, while Christ is the rescuer, literally the savior, who defeats this enemy and releases humankind from its imprisonment.

Satan appears in neither the Catechism nor the Creed. Although a character in all manifestations of the Christus Victor tradition, in the Catechism and the Creed he is "replaced" by evil, death, and sin. This is because the tradition of the undivided Church understands that evil, insofar as it concerns human beings, is a phenomenon within human experience, and that no supernatural agency is necessary to explain it.

Many Christians, perhaps most, have believed in the devil, in the existence of an objective, personal, intelligent, willfully evil being. Such a figure seems best able to explain the phenomenon of evil. Christian theology does not, however, focus on this fig-

ure, and does not depend on his existence for doctrinal logic.
The Creed does not, and the Catechism does not. The abstractions *sin, death,* and *evil* are not abstractions in human experience, and account for the existential situation we addressed in
the first chapter.

The scriptural and traditional witness to the devil is so strong,
however, that he is not absent from the liturgical tradition, certainly not from the Book of Common Prayer. In the prayer book
the devil appears in key liturgies, preeminently the baptismal
liturgy, which includes vows which reject Satan and his minions.[17]

In the twentieth century, which is closing, we may have begun
to appreciate anew the positive and healthy implications of the
Christus Victor theology, as we have come to appreciate many
pre-medieval theological values. We have not, however,
attempted to mitigate the tragic reality of Christ as the Lamb of
God *(Agnus Dei).* Since the Catechism includes both models of
atonement side by side, we can appreciate both models. Any
Christian is free to emphasize one or the other in devotional life.

The next question carries a good deal of theological weight as
the completion of the doctrine of the Incarnation. What do we
mean when we say Jesus "ascended into heaven"? We might
mean that we are affirming the tradition, reported in two Gospels,
that Jesus was lifted up into the skies when he left the disciples—either that day or forty days after the resurrection, depend-
ing on which tradition we prefer. The Catechism, however,
understands the Creed not as repeating the tradition but as inter-
preting it.

The Ascension is not "about" how Jesus left the earth, but is
"about" what became of the Incarnation—the Word made flesh.
Jesus took our human nature into heaven where he now reigns
with the Father and intercedes for us. Reference to direction is
carefully avoided. Heaven is not located above in any sense

---

17. This is, I believe, an illustration of the liturgical principle articulated
by the Belgian scholar Anton Baumstark, who pointed out that the most
solemn services tend to be most conservative in language and use. The earliest baptismal rites we know of contain dramatic renunciations of Satan and
his domain and involve turning to the West, the symbolic direction of dark-
ness and death, and spitting in Satan's face.

except the metaphorical, with "up" seeming to connote aspiration and exhilaration universally.

What is important is that human nature has been taken into heaven and that when Jesus left this existence and this earth, he remained human, retaining his flesh, emotions, and physical limitations. It may be fair to speculate that many Christians do not realize this, while others may grasp the concept intellectually but not imaginatively. The cosmic Christ, Christus Victor, Kristos Pantokrator, and similar triumphal visions of Christ, though valid theologically, have managed to obliterate the significance of the Ascension.

Depictions of the Ascension itself, which tend to be triumphalist in mode, have reinforced the problem. The Ascension is a moment of the elevation of the human, not an epiphany of heaven. It is meant, as the Catechism affirms, to assure us that our human nature has been admitted to the highest place, and that we have an intercessor in heaven, an advocate, a counselor. The same advocate, however, is coregent in heaven—he "reigns with the Father."

The next answer in a sense divides Catholic Christians from evangelicals and others. How do we share in his victory? "We share in his victory when we are baptized into the New Covenant and become living members of Christ." The evangelical answer would involve "accepting" Christ as one's Savior. Our tradition is less "intellectual," not involving assent to belief, but incorporation, which we believe enables us to share in this victory. Note carefully that the question is not, "How do we avoid eternal perdition?" It is far more positive, asking how we can be fellow victors, not survivors, in the spiritual combat.

This way of posing the question avoids in part the classic problem of what becomes of non-Christians. On this question, we find diversity of answers within the tradition, insofar as it is asked at all. Augustine believed that non-Christians are lost, and Cyprian stated that there was no salvation outside the Church. Origen, on the other hand, believed that God's love was so pervasive that literally nothing could stop it. Even the demons of hell—as creatures God made and therefore loved—would eventually find their way back into the Kingdom of Heaven. This doctrine is called *apokatastasis*, for which Origen was condemned but which has a certain life of its own, occurring from time to time throughout Christian thought.

Our catechetical emphasis on the corporate nature of redemption does not deny or denigrate the reality of individual salvation. The individual is still emphasized in our liturgical tradition, especially in the penitential season of Lent. Individual salvation is still stressed in hymns found in the current hymnal. On the principle of *lex orandi*, we affirm the salvation of the single lost soul every time we sing "Amazing Grace."

The overriding emphasis, however, is on the community rather than on the individual. That is what using the language of the New Covenant suggests—the Christian sense of being the new Israel, the Body of Christ, an eschatological community. These concepts all involve a communal sense or consciousness, rather than a distinctive individuality. Paradoxically, however, in an era which gives enormous lip service to individuality, admitting one's membership in such a community can seem strikingly individualistic and nonconformist.

In a sense, we are returning to the initial word in our theological journey: we. Who are "we"? We are the people of the new covenant, which is the essence of Christology. The Messiah arrived to establish, inaugurate, and forge it in the conscience. The new covenant, we now affirm, is the new relationship with God given by Jesus Christ, the Messiah, to the apostles; and through them, to all who believe in him. Like the old covenant, it is a relationship, primarily between us and God. But it is "new." The old relationship, we recall, was made with Israel, giving a particular vocation to a particular people. The new covenant is "like unto" it. Christians likewise have a peculiar relationship with God, which sets them apart from the rest of humanity. As in the case of the old Israel, this vocation does not involve superiority, privilege, or favor; it is a matter of fulfilling a task. All this is implicit in the New Testament, like virtually all theological material. The notion first become explicit in the early author known as Barnabas, writing probably in the middle of the second century. He or she writes an entire letter in which the Old Testament is taken, down to its most minute details, as a mirror image of the New Testament, predicting or adumbrating it in almost every verse.

Though the covenant does not involve privilege, it does involve promises on both sides. On the side of God, the promises are "to bring us into the kingdom of God and give us life in all its fullness." Covenant theology thus involves kingdom theology in the sense that we are guaranteed inheritors of God's kingdom. All this should not be strange to anyone familiar with the Gospels. It is the language Jesus uses whenever he talks about humankind and God. Two features should be underscored. First, as Jesus announces, the kingdom is "among" us. Inheritance of the kingdom is not a promise to be fulfilled at the death of the individual or at some unspecified future date, but immediately.

On the other hand, the kingdom, common sense tells us, is manifestly not among us. Traditionally, we say that it is not fully "inaugurated." It is simultaneously here and not here. The goal is achieved, yet remains distant. This difficult, nonrational aspect of our theology is called *realized eschatology*, meaning that the future is already here. Christ has brought us into God's kingdom already. In time, that truth will become clear, but for now we know it, minimally, by faith. These thoughts form part of what later tradition means by the term *Church militant*—present-day Christians struggling with the immanence of the kingdom, in the context of an often hostile cosmos. The *Church triumphant* will one day manifest what is now implicit.

Second, we do not affirm with Cyprian that there is no salvation outside the Church. We say that Christ has promised to bring us into the kingdom. We do not say that he will leave out those who do not share our identity. This realization is especially important in an age of theological pluralism and confusion. Christians now know, or realize with unprecedented vividness, two things that Cyprian did not know and our most recent forebears might not have known:

1. that a majority of persons now living are not Christians, and are not likely to become Christians; and

2. that the majority of human beings who lived in the past were also not Christians, and never had the option of becoming Christians.

We know now, for example, that the overwhelming majority of human beings lived before the time of Christ, and that only the smallest fraction of these were people of the Old Covenant. We know that Christianity is a minority religion in the present, and apparently one declining in numbers.

As many thoughtful people have insisted, it would fall between folly and evil to insist that this majority be excluded from God's kingdom due to something over which they have no control. This dilemma occurred to thoughtful Christians in the past, who lacked our numerical perspective, showing that it has always been difficult to attribute arbitrariness to God.

St. Augustine was probably the most rigorous proponent of an absolute spiritual dichotomy, of the chasm between heaven and hell, and his influence has always exerted dominance in the Western Church. But even he mitigated this doctrine profoundly with the notion of "baptism by desire," according to which anyone, including that vast majority who had never heard of Jesus Christ, could be admitted into the eschatological kingdom given a charitable disposition of soul.

The later Middle Ages, with Augustine's doctrine in mind, spoke of the *anima naturaliter christiana,* the "soul by nature Christian." Medieval authors used this concept to explain that beloved pagans, such as the epic poet Vergil, were "in heaven." Thus we speak of Christ's descent to "the dead," not qualifying or limiting that descent. We do not say that he descended to the Hebrews, or to the pre-Christian righteous. We do not believe that God excludes everyone but us. We affirm that we are included. At most, we may know what others may not.

This certainty[18] is included in the second part of the catechetical promise, "life in all its fullness." This is an apt translation of

---

18. I deliberately use a term—*certainty*—that Descartes introduced into modern philosophy. Experiments in qualifying philosophical claims derive ultimately from his work.

the words "eternal life," often taken to mean "life everlasting." The wry and intelligent Greek myth of Tithonus suggests the inadequacy of "life everlasting" as a human wish. Tithonus is granted that wish, but not everlasting vigor. He slowly degenerates into a human shell, with an insect-like existence and a voice begging for death.

By eternal life the tradition has always meant something positive, not the negative notion of life which does not cease. Here the imagination often fails even serious Christians. The imagery of heaven and the heavenly life—almost entirely postbiblical—has enforced the idea of a rarefied and disembodied existence, as the popular image of a saint has enforced the image of a committed Christian life as detached, removed from the physical. Christians have often recognized an absurdity in the heavenly visions offered by other theological systems, which seem to concentrate on a sensually attractive heaven. In place of this vision, Christianity too often offers an attenuated existence few people would choose.

The popular and traditional idea of heaven does not seem to reflect life in "its fullness." The standard heavenly iconography of clouds, wings, harps, and so on amounts to nothing but a modern corruption of medieval iconography. It may be objected that serious Christians do not believe in such ideas, but language betrays them. Even the most theologically sophisticated Christians resort to this imagery when speaking unguardedly. It is a matter of the imagination needing revision in the pictures it conjures of heaven. The problems in these pictures are compounded by a bizarre confusion of human beings and angels, two different orders of being according to Christian tradition. The image is of life attenuated, restricted, and enfeebled—the opposite of life fully realized.

The Gospel concept (or model) of the kingdom of God is, by contrast, completely robust and joyful. In Jesus' teaching and parables, the most common comparison is with a banquet, as at a family gathering or religious festival—the sort of experience people associate with "life in all its fullness." Further, the genuine Christian doctrine of bodily resurrection reinforces this image. A purely mental or spiritual existence for most people represents a nightmare, not a vision of heaven.[19]

The idea that the most refined existence is abstracted from the physical is Platonic, not Christian or Hebraic. Its rationale is expressed in Plato's most comprehensive work, the *Republic*, wherein control of the state is relegated to the most intellectually proficient members of society, and the body is pictured as a beast to be disciplined and controlled by the mind. Matter is depicted as rough, imperfect, deceptive, and evil.

The biblical idea, by contrast, is of a psychosomatic unity. Body, mind, and spirit, though distinguishable in theory,[20] are a unity in the human being. Our notion that Christ promised life in all its fullness depends on such unity. The notion means a life more unified than the fragmented and alienated existence we now experience, a life whose satisfactions are deeper and last longer.

But the word *now* from the previous statement must be qualified. Since the kingdom is in one sense already present, so the promise of the fullness of life must also be fulfilled. For this idea we have the witness of the conspicuous saints.[21] These saints are, in general, almost preposterously joyful persons. As G. K. Chesterton notes in *St. Francis of Assisi*, the genuine saint does not behave like a suffering ascetic but like a person "in love."[22] Being "in love" represents one of the most accessible examples of life lived to its fullest. People "in love," even at a young age and for the first time, really do experience colors and odors more vividly, think more rapidly, and experience higher highs and lower lows.

The human requirements of the covenant are spelled out in detail in the baptismal covenant, but are well summarized by the

---

19. Consider Samuel Beckett plays such as *Endgame, Happy Days*, and *Breath*, which capture the nightmarish quality of disembodied experience.

20. I mean "theory" in its root sense: "when you look at them," not in the sense of "when you play intellectual make-believe." Body, mind, and spirit are distinguishable the way the various components of the face are distinguishable, yet in a real sense inseparable parts of a single being.

21. By "conspicuous saints" I mean saints as distinguished from the New Testament sense of the word.

22. G. K. Chesterton, *St. Francis of Assisi* (New York: Image, 1957), p. 15.

catechetical statement that "Christ commanded us to believe in him and to keep his commandments." By "believe in" we mean *believe* in the fuller sense of the word, not the limited sense traced earlier of believing in a thing's existence. To "believe in" Christ means to stake everything on the reality and truth of his life and identity, on the great christological assertions implicit in the Gospels and proclaimed in the Creed.

This much is easy to understand. The second part of the assertion is more complex. Jesus asks Christians "to keep his commandments." Having already encountered the Ten Commandments in our anthropological reflections, we have realized that we cannot keep them. What are the commandments of Christ? If Christ "commanded us to keep them," do they fall into the same category as the former commandments, which serve ultimately to demonstrate our inability to keep them?

Christ's commandments are two, combining a summary of the law—"you shall love the Lord your God with all your heart, with all your soul, and with all your mind"—and the new commandment, "[to] love one another" as Christ loves us. They parallel the two segments of the Decalogue of love for God and love for fellow human beings. The two commandments raise problems and solve them.

The idea of a summary of law did not originate with Jesus but was commonplace in rabbinics. Given the sheer volume of legal material in the tradition—the rabbis counted more than six hundred laws in the Torah, and Judaism increasingly identified with them, as cult ritual became less and less operative—strict observance would seem unlikely if not impossible for most persons. One commonsense solution to that problem would be to summarize or to get at the "spirit" behind that plethora.

To Jesus, the love of God and love of the human being summed up the commandments. This summary can make the situation more, not less, difficult. Observing positive precepts can be far more daunting a task than observing prohibitions. Yet the Catechism presents these precepts as though they should be kept. They are "required" by Christ and seem to be offered in a pragmatic spirit as matters to be fulfilled, not as ideals that are never reached.

Everything previously asserted about *love* here finds its practical meaning. We asserted that Christian love was pragmatic, having to do with will—that it is instinctual, not affective. We asserted further that love is most clearly demonstrated by Jesus' death, which was, as all four Gospels agree, a willing death, dependent on Jesus' decision. Had Jesus not willed it, it could never have happened, despite Pilate, the Pharisees, and Satan. Of Jesus' feelings, of his emotional state, were are told nothing once his will is resolved in the Garden of Gethsemane.

Does this mean we are called to die like Christ? The answer is that we are called to follow the example of his will. The nature of Christ's example is mitigated by the example he gives in his new commandment. He says, "Greater love no one has than this, than to offer his life for another." But the prophetic action that follows is that of washing the disciples' feet.

– 6 –

Pneumatology

The world is charged with the grandeur of God.
  It will flame out, like shining from shook foil;
  It gathers to a greatness, like the ooze of oil
Crushed. Why do men then now not reck his rod?
Generations have trod, have trod, have trod;
  And all is seared with trade; bleared, smeared with toil;
  And wears man's smudge and shares man's smell: the soil
Is bare now, nor can foot feel, being shod.

And for all this, nature is never spent;
  There lives the dearest freshness deep down things;
And though the last lights off the black West went
  Oh, morning, at the brown bring eastward, springs—
Because the Holy Ghost over the bent
  World broods with warm breast and with ah! bright wings.

                              —G. M. HOPKINS, "GOD'S GRANDEUR"

Q. Who is the Holy Spirit?

A. The Holy Spirit is the Third Person of the Trinity, God at work in the world and in the Church even now.

Earlier we considered the traditional idea that God as Father, especially as Creator, is accessible to human reason. God's existence can be intuited, and reasonable, rational arguments can be made for God's existence. Then we explored the idea of Jesus Christ, God's Son, as revelation. As God's perfect image, Christ shows us more of God's nature. In different ways, then, the Father and the Son are for us expressions of God's nature. Therefore, most Christians and even nonbelievers have distinct impressions of God as Father, and of God as Son.

The Holy Spirit, whom we now begin to consider, has always seemed more elusive than the Father or the Son. Even nonreflective Christians tend to have a mental image of Jesus Christ, instilled by centuries of iconography. This is true even though we know next to nothing of the appearance of the earthly Jesus. Most have a less distinct visual impression of God the Father as well—usually as someone male, white, and old—though that image may be absurdly restricted and profoundly misleading.

More significant, most people have definite theological notions of the Father and Son, though these notions may be misleading or rudimentary God the Father is understood as the powerful, mysterious Creator, and, sometimes, as the stern, demanding Judge. God the Son is understood as the sacrificial Victim, and, sometimes, as the loving Friend and Brother. As with the visual icons, these are properly speaking "impressions" and "notions," not well-reasoned doctrine. They give a starting point for theology; they give meaning, however incomplete, to the phrases "God the Father" and "God the Son."

Such impressions do not exist for the Holy Spirit. For many, I suspect, the words are meaningless or barely meaningful. Most

Christians have no visual concept of the Holy Spirit. A few may associate the Spirit with the traditional iconography of the dove, but that is scarcely the same thing. A dove is a conventional symbol,[1] not a portrait. It no more depicts the Holy Spirit than the color blue suggests "life-threatening emergency," though every hospital worker learns to read blue that way. Since the Spirit is incorporeal (without body) and immaterial (without matter), lack of an associated image is to be expected.

The problem is that most have no theological concept of the Spirit, no real thought, feeling, attitude, or conviction about this aspect[2] of God. Persons may have vague notions of a doctrine about the Holy Spirit and, aside from the Nicene Creed, they may have impressions of a nonpersonal force. But no definite ideas will exist like the Father as Creator or the Son as Victim.

Most telling of all, whom do Christians address when they pray extemporaneously? Almost always they address "God," "Father," or "Jesus" and/or "Christ." How often is extemporaneous prayer in worship, not a liturgical prayer or hymn,[3] addressed to God the Holy Spirit? How often does a prayer begin, "Dear Holy Spirit" or "Creator Spirit, come dwell with us"? For most, the Spirit is nothing more than an "article of faith," a matter of words vaguely "adhered to," part of the linguistic trappings of worship, and part of the Creed. But the Spirit is not a part of their working theology, and not a living person.

Yet the Catechism and long-standing tradition call the Holy Spirit a person, and our liturgy is replete with such references. We will examine this deceptively familiar word *person* shortly, but for now our intuitive sense of what it means—a conscious individ-

---

1. A conventional symbol is an agreed-upon symbol, like the hexagon for "stop," which we all can read but which has nothing intrinsically to do with the act of "stopping."

2. The Holy Spirit is not, in Christian thought, an "aspect" of God. I am using the word provisionally, as we have not yet decided exactly "what" the Spirit is, what the Son is, or what the Father is.

3. An entire section of the 1982 hymnal is devoted to the Holy Spirit. But there is a distinct emotional difference between established and extemporaneous prayer. Formal prayers teach us, but despite the many formal prayers addressed to the Spirit, few of us have learned how to speak directly to her.

ual—will suffice. How in Christian practice do we relate to this person? Hymns address the Spirit directly, as in, "Come, gracious Spirit, heavenly dove." At the climactic moment in the Eucharistic liturgy, we ask God the Father to send the Holy Spirit upon the gifts of bread and wine, "that they may be" the body and blood of Christ.[4] The Creed itself asserts that the Holy Spirit is (1) God; (2) Lord; and (3) giver of life. Clearly, the Spirit is uniquely important, exalted, and equal to Father and Son. The question becomes why popular notions of the Spirit seem vague.

The simplest answer may be the most accurate. The Spirit seems vague not because of remoteness, but because of proximity. If the traditional doctrine reflected in our catechetical answer above is correct in assigning the Spirit to the present, quotidian life of the Church and world, then the Spirit—not Jesus—is God-with-us now, the new Emmanuel. Both the Father and the Son we can contemplate from a certain intellectual distance. We can ponder the cosmological argument in thoughtful repose and try to contemplate God the Son at the right hand of the Father in heaven. But the Holy Spirit, if doctrine is correct, is present now in a manner unlike the Son or Father. The Spirit is our divine medium, and it may be that we are unaware of the Spirit's presence even during moments when that presence is dynamic and decisive. We are vitally dependent on this medium, as we are on the air we breathe. The air bears life-giving oxygen, but we become aware of it only if there is a problem with the air or our lungs.

The Holy Spirit is difficult to discern, because the Sprit is our theological context. Though it might involve reading unintended meanings into the Creed, it is noteworthy that, according to a bit of justifiable eisegesis, mention of the "One, Holy, Catholic, and Apostolic Church," along with the resurrection of the dead and life of the world to come, appears in the paragraph headed by the Spirit. Church doors are painted red, the traditional color of the Spirit. The Spirit's prominence is such that it is worth our time to

4. The words in this case, are borrowed from Prayer B, but all four Eucharistic Prayers contain some version of this prayer, technically called the epiclesis.

develop a *pneumatology*—a theory of the Holy Spirit—just as we constructed a Christology better to understand God the Son.

This in many ways is the most difficult part of our exploration. As with any other theological experience, it is difficult for serious theology to come to grips with the Holy Spirit. The number of theological treatises on God or Jesus far outnumber those on the Spirit. God gave us the Son and the Word to explain God's self, but the Spirit does not exist for this purpose. At the same time, we have many hints as to the Spirit's identity.

If the Spirit is a present, proximate reality, and therefore difficult to "observe," it may be helpful to consider the historical impressions of Spirit contained in Scripture. The Hebrew word for spirit, *ruach*, which is identical to the word for "breath" and "wind," appears in the second verse of Genesis, when the "mighty wind" sweeps across the inchoate waters before creation. God's Spirit is often spoken of as an extension of God, or even as simply a way of saying that God is acting in a particular way. Psalm 51:11, for example, which contains the phrase "take not your holy spirit from me," can be understood according to a Christian interpretation. But it can just as easily mean, "be not far from me, O God." The language offers a memorable way of speaking, but is far from a doctrine of the Spirit as a person. Such scriptural examples present the Spirit as a "part" of God, as little more than a figure of speech. No separate or distinct identity for the Spirit is implied.

The question of the gender of the Spirit may seem to complicate these considerations. The Hebrew word is feminine, as is the Latin word *anima* (though *spiritus* is masculine, as is the Greek equivalent). Many have noted that the feminine identity preserves some suggestion of the feminine aspects of God, reinforced by actions attributed to the Spirit which seem conventionally feminine. Even more clearly than the case of the Father, however, the Spirit has no gender. We are in a quandary trying to decide on an appropriate pronoun. *It* seems to imply a blind and dumb force, such as Thomas Hardy trembled before in his poem "Hap"; to use either *he* or *she* tempts us to visualize a masculine- or a feminine-shaped ghost. Perhaps the best idea is not to visualize the Spirit at all. The best habit, linguistically, would be to alternate freely among pronouns, which is what we will do in this text.

We will in fact favor the feminine pronoun. If this choice seems strange initially, it can remind us that our theological imaginations have been incorrectly trained by linguistic habit. Calling the Spirit "she" is as theologically valid as "he," and better than "it." Given the almost inextricable masculinity of the Son and the somewhat more pliable masculinity of the Father, such usage can help achieve better anthropomorphic balance.[5]

The concept of the Spirit as a separate personality or entity first appears in narratives in which the Spirit of God descends upon, seizes, or somehow empowers individual human beings. These are warrior-leaders at first, such as Joshua, Gideon, and Samson. Samson's strength, for example, comes by means of the Spirit of Yahweh:

> Samson went down to Timnath and, when he reached the vineyards there, a young lion came at him growling. The spirit of the LORD suddenly seized him and, having no weapon in his hand, he tore the lion in pieces as if it were a kid. He did not tell his parents what he had done. (Judges 14:5–6, NEB)

Later, the prophets become the special domain of the activity of the Spirit. They are "inspired," filled with *ruach,* in order to utter God's words. Thus the Spirit of God seizes Isaiah, just as the Spirit seized Samson: "The spirit of the Lord GOD is upon me because the LORD has anointed me; he has sent me to bring good news to the humble, to bind up the broken-hearted, to proclaim

---

5. The entire question involves cultural assumptions about masculinity and femininity that should probably be questioned. Is aggressiveness an intrinsic characteristic of maleness? Are tenderness and nurture necessarily feminine? If not, what do the notions of masculinity and femininity represent, besides their physical functions? Rosemary Radford Reuther makes the same point in *To Change the World: Christology and Cultural Criticism* (New York: Crossroad, 1981). She writes that tradition tends to "abstract the human person as masculine and feminine into a dualism of opposite principles, masculinity and femininity. They give different valuations to each side. . . . This sets up an insoluble problem for human personhood until these qualities labeled masculine and feminine are seen as the product of social power relations rather than as 'nature'" (p. 55). In a real sense, masculinity and femininity do not exist.

liberty to captives and release to those in prison" (Isaiah 61:1, NEB). In the case of Isaiah and Samson, the person seems "possessed," taken over by another personality. An onlooker presumably could see that a strength other than Samson's performs his feats. A listener could hear that a voice other than Isaiah's is speaking the oracles. Samson and Isaiah are "not themselves." A distinct personality has displaced theirs. That distinctiveness is the genesis of the Christian doctrine of the Spirit as person.

In the first three Gospels, the synoptics, the Spirit is a distinct player in the dramas that unfold. In Matthew, the Spirit leads Jesus into the wilderness, departs, and comes again. In Luke, the Spirit is the agent of Mary's miraculous pregnancy. In Mark, the Spirit descends in the form of the dove upon Jesus at his baptism. The Spirit is not mentioned again as a visual manifestation until the opening of Acts, when she appears as fire and, echoing the Old Testament, as wind. We can say that the Spirit in these Gospels is as much a character as the human persons who take the stage.

In the Fourth Gospel, the most theologically developed of the four, the Spirit has less of a role. That suits John's theology perfectly, for he is interested in the career of the Word as distinct from the Spirit. Like Luke, John sees the Spirit as a later arrival. "The Spirit had not yet been given, because Jesus had not yet been glorified" (John 7:39, NEB). John understands the Spirit as the Comforter, as the "replacement" for Jesus Christ, who will appear only after Jesus' passion. In the "farewell discourses" of Jesus, from John 13–15, the most distinct Gospel theology of Spirit, Son, and Father as separate "entities" appears, as Jesus, the Word of God and Son, refers to his Father repeatedly, then concludes with a promise of the Spirit as the Advocate (14:26, 15:26), teacher (14:16), and comforter (14:16).

Matthew 28:19, in which Jesus commands his disciples to baptize "in the name of the Father and the Son and the Holy Spirit," goes further. The verse contains the only three-part reference to Father, Son, and Spirit in the Gospel tradition. Scholars attribute the saying to the developing Church, doubting strongly that Jesus himself had such a developed theology. But use of the phrase would still mean that, by the time the Gospel of Matthew was written, within thirty to forty years of the death of Jesus, the Church had already come to understand God as Father, Son, and Holy Spirit. The Church thus made such usage, as in baptism, central to the faith.

In the Book of Acts, the Spirit becomes the central character, replacing Jesus. The subject of the book is the action of the Spirit in taking the Church from Jerusalem to Rome, from its Judaic matrix into the ecumenical world. The book begins with the quintessential act of inspiration, as the Holy Spirit descends upon the nascent Church in tongues of flame. "A sound came from heaven like the rush of a mighty wind, and it filled all the house where they were sitting. And there appeared to them tongues as of fire, distributed and resting on each one of them. And they were all filled with the Holy Spirit and began to speak in other tongues, as the Spirit gave them utterance" (Acts 2:2–4, RSV). This episode takes place during the Jewish summer festival of wheat ingathering, called "Pentecost" in Greek. The festival came fifty days after Passover, and therefore the Christian feast day of the Holy Spirit, arriving fifty days after the resurrection, has been called Pentecost ever since.

Its theological significance is enormous and often underestimated. For the first time we can speak of an eccesiological event, of an event in the history of the Church. The Church had come into being. During the earthly ministry of Jesus depicted in the Gospels there was no Church. The disciples followed a single, inspired leader, Jesus, who has the Holy Spirit in all four Gospels while the others do not. He alone is the charismatic leader. At Pentecost, the Spirit is bestowed upon the Church as a whole. Early Christians noted that, as a general outpouring of the Spirit had been predicted by Ezekiel (36:26) and Jeremiah (31:31) as a characteristic of the messianic age, the event represented a completion of the ministry of Jesus. The tongues of flame rested upon all the disciples, not just a leader or a group of leaders. The Spirit did not just rest on those who might be called "clergy." The wind apparently was heard by all, not by the select few. Even at Jesus' baptism, apprehension of the Spirit seems to have been a private affair. Jesus saw the Spirit but the others did not. But after Pentecost the Holy Spirit became the general source of strength and guidance for the Church that Jesus had promised. The Old Covenant mode of granting leadership to charismatic individuals was over.

Such notions of the Spirit do not appear in St. Paul's thought. This does not mean that he was unaware of such thinking. Paul's letter-writing ministry was restricted to specific groups under specific circumstances, as many readers fail to realize. Thus, he does not deal with the question of charismatic inspiration. Paul does seem to assume the general inspiration of the churches under the aegis of the Holy Spirit. He does not add much beyond that statement, probably because there is not much to say. Regarding his theological understanding of the Spirit, Paul in his letters demonstrates a theology and a pneumatology in a state of development. Paul speaks variously of Father and Son, of Father, Son, and Spirit, of the Spirit of the Son, and so on. He has not formulated a three-part theology like the Creed's. Paul seems to know "the difference" between Father and Son and Spirit, but he does not explain it systematically.

The same fluid quality appears in the first Christian writings outside the New Testament, customarily called the Apostolic Fathers.[6] In the letter of Clement, the letter of Barnabas, the letters of Justin Martyr, and the *Didache*, all written before the year 150, the Holy Spirit is a distinct reality. The Spirit is never fixed in relationship to the Son and the Father. As in Paul, the question of defining this relationship never seems to have occurred to these authors.

Why did the question ever come up? Why was it necessary, by the time the ecumenical Creed was invented in the fourth century, to try to state precisely the relationship among Father, Son, and Spirit, and to delineate at length the Spirit's nature and (in 381) her operations? The answer to this question is not a matter of theological history, but relates to the very nature of the Spirit.

---

6. This name, coined in the seventeenth century, usually refers to all Christian writings, besides those in the New Testament, written in the first century after the death of Jesus. Most are pseudonymous or anonymous, and none were written by associates of the apostles.

In the latter part of the second century, Christian groups loosely associated under the priest Montanus were claiming peculiar, private, and highly particular manifestations of the Holy Spirit. They were the first in a long historical line of charismatic Christians, whose common denominator is posing such claims. The implication is often that they have replicated, emended, or replaced the original experience of Pentecost, that there has been a new illapse of the Spirit, of which they have been the special beneficiaries, and that they are entitled to a new status within the Church, or to form a new community replacing the Church.

The dangers of this scenario, and its refutation of the Book of Acts, are obvious. The Montanists, however, like many charismatic groups since, reinforced their claims with more spectacular spiritual activities, such as talking in tongues or *glossolalia*—the sort of spiritual pyrotechnics about which wiser heads such as Paul had always been cautious (see First Corinthians).

A clear-cut doctrine of the Holy Spirit was necessary. Up to this point, references to the Holy Spirit are almost exclusively experiential. Almost no attention is given to defining the Spirit or to understanding her nature. An emphasis on relation begins to appear alongside but never displaces the emphasis on function, as the question of exactly "what" and "who" this Spirit might be begins to seize Christian minds. The problem of distinguishing between Father and Son, which we examined in the section on Christology, was compounded by Christians' sense of the Holy Spirit as a third divine reality. Gradually, a way of naming that reality, and of expressing both Christian theological intuition and Christian experience of the living God, came into focus.

The difficulty for the early Church, and for Christians ever since, was in making sense of the three distinct realities Christians had come to know as Father, Son, and Holy Spirit, while doing justice to the equally powerful doctrine and conviction of the oneness of God. The first ways of expressing the three realities—God in three roles, God in three aspects, God in three modes of expression—seem initially to make sense, but upon further reflection will not prove sufficient. When we say of a human being, "She is really several people: a wife, a mother, a lawyer, and a member of the vestry," we are speaking in metaphors. She is not several different people, she is one. When she "plays the role" of lawyer, she is still presumably recognizable to child, husband, and other vestry members as the "same" human being with whom they have a relationship. *Aspect*, which means surface appearance, is weaker still, as are its synonyms. *Mode* is a more abstract and mechanistic way of saying "role." None of these ideas, in short, implies enough separation among the three entities.

On the other hand, the other alternatives—God as three beings, three individuals, three divinities—all err in the other direction. They imply too much separation, suggesting that God is not "one God" as we asserted at the beginning. They carry Christianity into polytheism and make the break with Judaism more radical and dangerous than it ever was meant to be. The Son and the Father, for example, were understood to be distinct, but not in the way sons and fathers in ordinary experience are distinct. Again, we might resort to the idea of family members, who are distinct yet remain "one." But family members are not one in the sense that Son and Father are one.

Between these arguments seemed to rest an "excluded middle." Every term either expressed too much distinctiveness or not enough individuality. For every new metaphor there would be second thoughts and exceptions. In the fifth century, for example, St. Patrick allegedly compared Father, Son, and Spirit to a shamrock, one plant with a single life but three distinct leaves. Yet the leaves are "attached" and are in no sense "individuals" the way the Spirit and the Son seem to be individuals.

The poverty of language and imagination on this question provides a good clue to the reality. We can only express in language what we understand. The linguistic truism that all language is metaphor expresses this idea. Any new idea must be compared to something already in existence. While we may intuit "what we mean" by an entity that is three and yet one, there is nothing else in our experience that contains simultaneously this degree of separation and unity. This theological concept is what we earlier called a primary reality. Like the color blue or the taste of a lime, it cannot be defined, only pointed toward.

But that pointing can be done. We can point toward the taste of a lime by saying that it is simultaneously sour and bitter, unlike that of a lemon. We can point toward the triune reality of God, and that is what the Church eventually did, providing the source of our traditional theological language.

"The Holy Spirit is the Third Person of the Trinity. . . ." (Book of Common Prayer, 852)

This assertion introduces for the first time two of the terms the Church gradually came to use to express both the Christian theological intuition and the Christian experience of the living God: *Person* and *Trinity*. Neither term appears in the ecumenical Creed,[7] and neither occurs in Holy Scripture. God acts as a "person" in Scripture, but not as Father or Son or Spirit. The terms were used in conciliar statements and creeds subsequent to Nicea and Constantinople, and soon attained an authority almost as great as that of the Creed. It is important nonetheless to remember that the terms are neither biblical nor creedal, and that they are very much examples of the "model" and "theory" aspects of theological expression examined above.

Person is the more difficult and misleading of the two words. Reflection suggests that all speakers of English have an intuitive sense of its meaning. Still, the word is notoriously difficult to define, yet indispensable when trying to understand the Holy Spirit. Definitions of Father and Son as divine realities are no longer possible now that we have introduced the third reality. Therefore, we must examine *Person* and *Trinity* before continuing with our pneumatology.

In English, the word *person* is practically a synonym for "human being." What is meant if you say, "My dog is my favorite person"? You have said nothing illogical in terms of biology, but you have violated common language, which restricts the word to human beings. A current *Webster's Collegiate Dictionary* confirms this impression by listing seven definitions for the word. Five

---

7. Both terms can be found in the so-called Athanasian Creed, included in our Book of Common Prayer among the historical documents. It is a useful statement, but has been rejected as a statement of doctrine.

definitions refer to human beings, one to the Christian tradition we are in the process of explaining, and one to the biological sense of the word. It would be impossible to explain the Christian faith with the phrase "God in Three Persons," without extending or altering the ordinary sense of the word *person*.

In the early Church, two words existed for the three differing divine realities, neither of which was *person*.[8] The Father, Son, and Spirit were called either *hypostases* or *prosopa* of God, Greek terms with different textures. *Hypostasis* is made up of the two Greek words for "under" and "stand" (or "exist"). The word thus meant "that which exists independently of other things, a definite individual," whether human or nonhuman, whether animal or inorganic. It could also refer to a definite location, nature, or "confidence."

The word *prosopon*, by contrast, was simple and definite, meaning "face." The multiple experience of God was expressed using one of these two words. Either God seemed to be three independent, individual entities or showed three different faces. The latter is the more visually impressive term, but the former prevailed and became the traditional language of the Church.

The term *hypostasis*, though complex, conveys the intended meaning. The Father, Son, and Spirit seemed distinct, seemed to be individuals. The term *prosopon* suggested a being with three faces, like certain representations of the Hindu Shiva. It was hardly an improvement over expressions describing "aspects," "features," or "modes" of God. *Prosopon* further reminded believers of the "personality" of God, that God is caring and compassionate, but it was too easy to visualize something misleading. Primary realities that are invisible always present this difficulty with visual symbols.

When the word *hypostasis* was translated into Latin, however, there was an immediate problem. The exact Latin equivalent had already been used to translate the idea the unity, the oneness, of God. Therefore, a word related to the concept of proso-

---

8. For a detailed analysis, see G. Prestige, *God in Patristic Thought*, chaps. 8–9.

pon was selected: *persona*. The word means "mask," literally "that which the sound comes through," since, in the ancient world, masks served as microphones and makeup.

The translators of the Creed did not mean to imply that God wore three masks, though classical masks—in contrast to the modern idea of mask that conceals—were meant to disclose and magnify the character. By the fourth century, the meaning of the word had gradually shifted. First, it shifted to mean "role," as in the "persona" in a play. Then it came to stand for "the part anyone plays in real life"—the "roles" humans assume, as in our example of the mother-wife-lawyer-churchwoman above. The word then shifted to mean the "person in the abstract," what we call the personality. But the term was more concrete, indicating the human being in the role and not just the role itself.

The word indicated in fifth-century Latin a tension between the abstract and the concrete, exactly what was wanted in defining the "person" of the divine being. It was a fortunate word choice at the time, and worked well in English as long as people also studied Latin. Like the word *very*, which meant "truly" or "in reality" when first used in Elizabethan English to translate the Creed, its meaning had shifted entirely, but knowledge of Latin made people aware of the original meaning. To count on knowledge of Latin today would be folly. *Person* now means one thing. As noted, the word now means "human being" and serves as a synonym for "man" or "woman." If we wish to understand the Catechism and the tradition it represents, we have to adjust our thinking in this crucial case.

Trinity is not nearly as difficult. It is the first theological word coined in Latin rather than in Greek or Hebrew, and is accessible because of a construction similar to English. Latin was adept at making simple abstract words, such as *Romanitas*, out of nouns. These abstract words indicated "the essential quality of the noun," its essence. In Late Latin, one could speak of the "thisness" and the "thatness" of a thing.

Trinity is the precise English equivalent of the Latin *Trinitas*—not a translation, but the word spelled differently in a new language. It was coined by a brilliant second-century Christian priest, Tertullian, who began his public career as a Roman lawyer, and therefore had a capacious and agile mind—the two qualities necessary for mastering the bulk and complexity of Roman law.[9] *Trinity* was a natural coinage for such a person and caught exactly the concept of three distinct individuals who share a single being.

"Being" is what the tradition insists that they share. The council of Chalcedon explicated this idea at length, but it is already contained in the Creed, which stipulates that the Son is "one Being" with the Father. The abstraction *Trinity* works where all the other models fail. A shamrock, which, according to legend, was St. Patrick's symbol for the Trinity, is one being and not three individuals. A man who is son, employer, and best friend is one being, but not three persons. On the other hand, three people working in close harmony are three, but are only "one" metaphorically. A talented horseback rider may seem to be "one" with the horse, but will fool no one except those who do not know horses.

The intriguing aspect about the word *Trinity* is that this Latin abstraction, invented by a lawyer, is one of the few words in our experience that stands for one entity. There is only one trinity in the universe, *the* Trinity. Any entity other than the divine Trinity fails either at oneness or at threeness.

That unity, later tradition affirmed, is a unity of being. The Creed contains a hint in asserting that the Son is "of one Being with the Father." "Being" in this case does not mean "entity" or "individuality," as it sometimes means in English. This meaning would contradict the idea of three persons. Rather, *Being* means "common existence" and relates more with the verb *to be* than with the corresponding noun. It translates the Greek word *ousia*, which meant the act of being, of existing. This makes the word a perfect correlative to the mythic name *Yahweh*, which evades exact translation but must mean something like "I am who exists." It is this *ousia*, this be-ing, that Father, Son, and Holy Spirit have in common. They share a divine life.

---

9. He concluded his career as a member of the Montanist schismatics, yearning for a more passionate expression of Christian realities.

When the Creed was translated into Latin, the word chosen for "Being" was *substantia*, which meant "something that can stand alone." The word could have been used to translate *hypostasis* as well. But it had already become common practice to think of *substantia* as the equivalent of the Greek word *ousia*, (the Roman thinker Cicero, for example, uses *substantia* when he speaks of the Greek Aristotle's teachings on *ousia*), and so it was a natural choice. Later, *substantia* was brought into English translations, which was unfortunate as the word *substance* took on a more restricted meaning in English. The word came to mean "material stuff" or "physical matter," and the creedal formula "being of one substance with the Father" suggested to generations of English-speaking peoples that Father and Son both were drawn from divine plasm. *Substance* is a "materialistic" word. Thinking in these terms would take us back to the pre-Socratic philosophers, who sought a material "substance" (water, air, fire) out of which everything else was made. *Being* is far closer to the spirit of the original than substance.

The Catechism affirms that the Spirit is God "at work in the world and in the Church even now." This is the reason for the immanence of the Holy Spirit mentioned earlier: the Holy Spirit is the Presence of God. Calling the Spirit a "person," given the particular meaning given that term, helps us to understand the distinction. The unity of God, at the same time, enables us to say that "God is with us" or that "Jesus is here" whenever we invoke the Holy Spirit.

The Creed and the Catechism both assert that the Spirit is "giver of life." The Creed adds that the Spirit is "Lord." The lordship of the Spirit reminds us that the Spirit shares authority over us and all creation with the Son and the Father.[10] Everything said about Christ's lordship applies equally to the Spirit—she, too, is our Lord, the head of our earth-household and our protector. The lordship of Christ and the Spirit counter any tendency we might have to exalt the Father over the other two, as if the Father were more truly "God" than Spirit or Son.

---

10. Cf. the discussion of the word Lord above.

The Holy Spirit is distinguished by being named the "giver of life." The Spirit, we claim, causes all animation and movement, whether of bodies or of mind. This idea is called the *animating principle*. From a Christian point of view, this is what Aristotle intuited when he argued for an ultimate "prime mover," a powerful but also intelligent and willful One who causes all other things to move and think. The same concept is expressed mythically in Genesis 2:7, in which Yahweh "formed a man from the dust of the ground and breathed into his nostrils the breath of life" (NEB). With the divine spirit-breath-wind, God "animates" the human and brings him to life.

Sallie McFague has pointed also to the consistency of this aspect of the Holy Spirit with twentieth-century science, one of the subthemes throughout this study. "[T]he model of God as spirit, the giver and renewer of her body, the universe, is one that is compatible with readings of both Christianity and postmodern science."[11] This statement also supports the notion that the Spirit is the most feminine aspect of God.

The Creed, though not the Catechism, further asserts that the Spirit "proceeds from the Father and the Son" and that, along with them, the Spirit "is worshipped and glorified." The second assertion is fairly simple to understand. Like calling the Spirit "Lord," worship helps guarantee full divine status, full equality with Father and Son. In the course of an eighth-century controversy regarding the use of images in worship,[12] it was pointed out that only God is the proper object of worship. Giving worship, or *latreia*, to anything else is to make that thing an idol and therefore to engage in idolatry. Conversely, to give the Holy Spirit anything less than worship is to deny the Spirit divinity—to make her less than God.

The "procession" of the Holy Spirit from Father and from Son is a different matter. The issue provoked immeasurable hostility

---

11. Sallie McFague, *The Body of God: An Ecological Theology* (Minneapolis: Fortress, 1993), p. 137.

12. The problem was to reconcile the use of images with the incorporeal nature of God, and, to some extent, with the third commandment.

and contributed to the schism between the Western and Eastern branches of the Church which exists to this day. Most Eastern theologians thought that to think of the Spirit as proceeding from both Father and Son reduced the Spirit, making her subsidiary to both. Western Christianity held, on the contrary, that procession of the Spirit guaranteed the loving communication between Father and Son. A compromise, endorsed by theologians such as John of Damascus in the East and Thomas Aquinas in the West, was that the Spirit proceeds from the Father through the Son, which seemed a happy solution. At any rate, the original idea had been the dynamic nature of the Trinity, that God is not static, that God "is a verb, not a noun." The tragedy was to reduce this concept to the meaning of prepositions, which are notoriously fluid and evasive.

All attempts to define the precise domain of any person of the Trinity run this risk. As we explore the aegis of the Spirit, following the Nicene Creed, we need to bear this caveat in mind. The Christian God is dynamic, not static, and while it makes sense to assert that the Holy Spirit is God "at work . . . even now," it also makes sense, to take two examples from ordinary prayer, to say that Jesus is "with us," or to ask God the Father to "be our guest." Traditional theology called this idea the *perichoresis* or *circumincession* of the three persons, which literally means their "moving around." For example, we can speak of the creative works of Spirit, Word, and Father. The priest-poet John Donne expressed it well in one of his "Holy Sonnets":

> Batter my heart, three-personed God, For you as yet but knock,
> breathe, shine, and seek to mend . . .

The question is, which person knocks? Scripturally, it is Jesus. Yet traditionally, the Father is mentioned first. Which breathes? The Spirit. Yet this verb is second. And which shines? The Son? The Father? On reflection, we realize that any of the three persons can be associated with any of these verbs—a poetic realization of *perichoresis*.

The Trinity, though an abstraction, is a doctrine of the dynamic nature of God. The three persons are fluid, kinetic, and interchangeable in their operations. With that warning in mind, we can investigate the dominion and operation of the Spirit, according to the Creed and Catechism.

First, "[the Spirit] has spoken through the prophets." We have already noticed that, in the Old Testament, the Spirit comes into clearest focus when inspiring the prophets. More is asserted in this statement. The divine inspiration for the Old Testament is guaranteed in a limited way. The term prophets is synecdoche for the entire Old Testament. The part substitutes for the whole, as in "all hands on deck."

Second, we believe in one, holy, catholic, and apostolic Church. We will explore this notion fully as we develop an ecclesiology. At this point is it important to note the special relationship of Spirit to Church. The great scholar-theologian of the third century, Origen, even contrasted the creativity of Christ, as the *Logos* who shaped the cosmos in general, with that of the Spirit, the Comforter, who shaped the Church. The Christian Church is traditionally the Spirit's domain, and it is one of the strange aspects of Church history that few local parish churches are named for the Holy Spirit. Many are named for Christ, Mary, and saints—or even for the abstract Trinity.

The third catechetical statement mentions baptism. The Spirit is called down upon the person in baptism, and upon the bread and wine at the Eucharist, in ways that are deliberately parallel.

Finally, we acknowledge the Spirit's dominion over the resurrection, and the life of the world to come. This acknowledgment reflects the symmetry and logic of the statement in the Nicene Creed. If the Spirit is Lord and giver of life, it is good sense that the Spirit should preside over resurrection and the life to come.

Before leaving this subject, let us consider the poem which serves as the preface to this chapter, Gerard Manley Hopkins's "God's Grandeur." Hopkins was a Victorian professor of classics and a member of the Jesuit order, and lived, by all accounts, a fairly conventional and modest life. In his poetry, however, he was a startling innovator. He anticipated the great poetic experiments of the twentieth century by several decades, and, as even this small sample suggests, was wrenching word order and meter into strange and unexpected patterns—all for the purpose of expressing meanings he could not express in a more conventional way.

He applies his *charism*, that talent of the spirit, again and again to the expression of his theology, which was similarly advanced. This poem—technically it is a sonnet—expresses many of the characteristics of the Holy Spirit we have touched on, and many of the preoccupations of later theology. Hopkins contrasts the fallen nature of humanity, which he characterizes as masculine, with the tender, sensitive, and yet definitely stronger presence of the Holy Spirit, which is also God the Creator and God the Redeemer. The poem serves as a fitting conclusion to our consideration of the divine person closest to us, close like the air we breathe.

-7-
The End of All Our Exploring

Love, like Matter
Is stranger than we thought.

—W. H. AUDEN

As noted throughout this work, theology is often provoked— challenged into existence by heresy, by controversies within the Church, and by changes and advances in secular thought and learning. With the closing of the twentieth century, we thus find ourselves in a classic theological predicament. We hear unanswered questions and look back upon uncharted territories: the three-pronged assault of Planck, Einstein, and Heisenberg on classical modern science; the bewildering course of modern philosophy, circumscribing human reason with a vengeance unknown to Locke, Berkeley, and Hume; the fantastic course of the modern arts, veering feverishly from Picasso to Joyce to Eliot to Schoenberg and Stockhausen through a myriad of expressions; and the startling, often shocking, tragedy of twentieth-century history. All developments have been taken, explicitly or implicitly, to point to the obsolescence, the irrationality, and the unsuitability of Christian faith.

The underlying thesis of this work has been that Christianity is affirmed by these seemingly disparate phenomena. Admittedly, the Church can be and has been used as a nostalgic retreat from contemporary reality, but classical Christian theology can offer something more substantial. It can make sense of the unconscious, can accept the principles of indeterminacy and of the space-time continuum, and can affirm the tragicomic aesthetics of *Ulysses* and *The Waste Land*.

It can make use of twentieth-century philosophy. That is one reason I have applied the methods of Ludwig Wittgenstein, considered almost antithetical to religious thought in the past. In his deceptively simple analyses of ordinary language, as the thought-experiments of Einstein are deceptively simple, Wittgenstein at first seemed to sound the death knell of metaphysics, and himself abandoned philosophy as a dead end for several years. In his later thought, however, Wittgenstein reexamined language and intuited its larger possibilities. He came to face the paradox of language as a way of expressing the ineffable. My work applies his suggestions.

I have chosen quotations from the *Four Quartets*, another poetic sequence by T. S. Eliot, as the epigram at the beginning of this book, and as the title for the last chapter. "The end of all our exploring / will be to arrive where we started. . . ." I believe this statement to be, among other things, a précis for theological work. Theology through the centuries has always involved a paradoxical dynamic of change within permanence, permanence within change. It has always been the river into which the pre-Socratic thinker Herakleitos invites us to step. Whenever the remarkable mental capacities of human beings, the God-given creativity and reason, have led to discovery and a change in worldview, theology has affirmed that "this, we have always known."

The postmodern scientific and philosophical world with its time-space continuum, indeterminacy, chaos theory, and acceptance of paradox is hardly strange to Christianity. Nor is it incompatible with the God of Scripture or inconsistent with the teachings of Jesus. Theology helped prepare us for the modern world. The wonder now is rather how Christianity ever seemed congruent with the hierarchical and militaristic worldview of the high Middle Ages, the nationalistic worldview of the Renaissance, or the nineteenth-century myth of progress.

I have referred frequently to the work of twentieth-century science. I offer one final example of the curious way in which twentieth-century scientific thought might prepare us for theology. Scripture, as skeptics have pointed out for centuries, is self-contradictory. Leaving aside the wrongheadedness involved in taking a virtual library of books like the Bible and demanding the logical consistency of a single volume, the point is a good one. The biblical record contradicts itself often. This is obviously true in matters of fact. There are different answers within the Bible to all these questions: What is the name of the man who killed the Philistine Goliath? What were the last words of Jesus Christ?

What were the names of the twelve disciples? Biblical scholarship can account for these contradictions.

The deeper problem is with matters of theology, for here, too, the scriptural record is inconsistent. For example, what is God "like"? What is the nature of God? It is a fundamental theological question. Theologians have given various answers, as does the Bible, picturing God as stern and unbending, as pliant and mild. The Bible tell us variously that God forgets sins and that God remembers sins forever. God is masculine and motherlike. God is utterly Other and intimately present. There is no explaining away that the nature of God is viewed inconsistently.

Tradition mirrors this inconsistency. Christian teaching from Augustine to Aquinas to Schleiermacher, for example, has affirmed as a central tenet the impassibility of God. Simultaneously, Christianity has taught that God is love. The theologians we have listed make this very point, thus, seemingly, contradicting themselves. The modern Jewish theologian Abraham Heschel, in his seminal work combining biblical scholarship with theological reflection, *The Prophets*, insists that the authentic scriptural understanding of God makes no room for the doctrine of impassivity, that God feels and suffers—not in an analogical sense, but actually. Recent theologians such as Kazo Kitamori have developed this idea further. So we have, in essence, two contradictory claims: that God is above suffering and that God suffers. God cannot be both, according to traditional logic.

But modern experience has shattered traditional logic, with twentieth-century physics providing a striking example. In 1927, Werner Heisenberg presented one of the most radical principles of modern physics, the "indeterminacy principle," which is now virtual scientific dogma. Newtonian physics had always assumed the measurability and the predictability of material reality, and thus had fostered the conviction that, given enough knowledge, the human mind could predict any physical phenomenon. Seventeenth- and eighteenth-century philosophers, in turn, sought similar explanations for nonmaterial reality such as ethics and metaphysics. These explorations achieved various levels of success and failure, but Newton's science was, until the twentieth century, accepted as a comprehensive, rational account of all physical reality.

Heisenberg made perhaps the most radical break with this modern scientific and philosophical tradition. He shattered Newtonian certainty by asserting that, at the subatomic level, particles were indeterminate—if we know the speed of an electron, we cannot know its location, and vice versa. The verb must be emphasized. If we *know* one fact we cannot *know* the other. Uncertainty, in other words, is certain. Similarly, physics has realized that light has two natures. On the one hand, it is a continuous wave; on the other hand, it is a series of discrete particles. This violates a principle once held as self-evident—that a thing cannot be two different things. It is staggering to our minds to discover that there are instances in which a clear principle has proven demonstrably false.

Reality, then, in two fundamental aspects, is paradoxical: these are not simply matters of "two different ways of looking" at some phenomenon, but rather phenomena that appear to be two mutually exclusive sorts of things: their own opposites, things that are simultaneously thesis and antithesis. They are impossible to understand in any normal logical way; our minds have to grasp them by the mix of imagination and will that we call faith (their proof, which is a matter of equation and experiment, is another question altogether).

Postmodern logical theory has allowed precisely the same thing. Until very recently, the logic Aristotle outlined in the fourth century before Christ was considered definitive: nobody was ever going to extend or challenge it, as Aristotle had said essentially all there was to say. But just as Copernicus and Kepler deposed a geocentric astronomy in the seventeenth century, Newton advanced mathematics beyond Euclid in the eighteenth, and Einstein enlarged physical science beyond Newton in the twentieth, so contemporary philosophy has at last challenged Aristotle. And a small but very real example of this challenge is the acceptance of contradictories: that realities that are apparently their own opposites can co-exist; that true paradoxes can exist. Not apparent paradoxes, not conundrums, but real instances where x = y and y = x.

The paradoxes of Christianity have always been of this sort. How can an omnipresent God be present as his own Son, who is also fully God? More simply, how can Christ simultaneously be "true God" and "truly human"? The tension in this theological principle is between transcendence and immanence. As John Macquarrie remarks, in his *Twentieth-Century Religious Thought*, twentieth-century "realist" theologians and metaphysicians have divided on this issue. The radical realist theologians, such as Teilhard de Chardin, posit a God "in process, . . . who in one way or another is not yet complete in his perfection."[1] The traditionalists "definitely put God beyond the spatiotemporal world." Macquarrie further observes that the former representation "is the more satisfying intellectually, and the one that is most consistent with the realist approach to metaphysics." He adds that the metaphysicians present "the more satisfying [proposal] religiously, though by placing God beyond space and time in some superempirical realm it throws away [the] virtues of realist metaphysics."

If a electron can be indeterminate and light simultaneously wave and particle—two categories which appear mutually exclusive—why cannot the same be true of God? Why can God not be both transcendent and in process? We cannot see how these two notions could be true simultaneously; but our understanding of light has taught us to accept such a paradox. Tradition and Scripture both speak of a God who is (1) immutable, impassible, "utterly Other," and transcendent; and (2) mutable, passible, "closer than a brother," and immanent.

Notice now that I do not intend to argue from analogy but to make a point about learning from physics. The latter science, at least since the eighteenth century, taught us to suspect contradictions and paradoxes as signs of flawed reasoning. Contemporary physics, on the contrary, teaches us to see paradox as pointing to ultimate reality. Newtonian physics do not "work" on a large or small scale, nor does Aristotelian logic. It should scarcely come as a surprise, then, that ultimate reality as viewed by philosophy should be similarly illogical. The reaction of mod-

---

1. Macquarrie, *Twentieth-Century Religious Thought*, p. 278.

ern philosophy was to retreat from ultimate questions, which had been philosophy's traditional subject matter. This retreat was in part an admission of limit. It lies behind Wittgenstein's retreat from saying the unsayable. But decades of modern consciousness have conditioned us to the paradoxical. If we can accept that light is and is not a wave, we can accept that God is impassible and that God loves.

A final question remains, one that we cannot answer. But we may begin to point a direction. Theology is consistent with twentieth-century science and thought, but is it consistent with postmodern history, with Hiroshima and Auschwitz, with the Jewish Holocaust and the Black Holocaust? That is the question of *theodicy*. How can we trust and believe in a loving and potent God given the reality of human suffering? The question has always been with us, but the twentieth century has magnified its significance to an unprecedented level of terror.

New Testament scholars assure us that even in their most primitive state, the Gospels affirmed that God is love. If by that word with many meanings we insist on a concept easily grasped and readily understood, then Christianity fails. But if we understand with Auden that love, like matter, has turned out to be far different and more difficult than we expected, then we can find in it the most daring, the most vital, and the most realistic of doctrines for the postmodern world.

You and I find ourselves in a classic theological predicament. The world has challenged us as Christians, and demands serious and honest response as it has throughout history. It is an uncomfortable position, but it has often provoked vital theology. Justin, in the second century, was faced with reconciling Christian faith with Classical thought; Anselm, in the eleventh, was confronted with the making of medieval Europe; in the High Middle Ages, Aquinas was challenged by the recovery of Aristotle; Luther and Zwingli in the sixteenth century were faced with the rise of modernity with all its critical skepticism; Joseph Butler in the eighteenth was challenged by Deism; the Oxford reformers in the nineteenth were challenged by Erastian complacency. Every defiant counter movement, every philosophical irritant, has provoked solid and unprecedented understanding of and articulation of our very Scriptures, Creeds, and tradition. Such challenges, to paraphrase Auden's epitaph for William Butler Yeats, have "hurt us into theology."

Above all, we find ourselves in the position of Augustine in the early fifth century. Challenged philosophically by eclectic Neoplatonism, he responded with *On the Trinity* and the *Confessions*. Challenged culturally by the achievements of Rome, he responded with *On Christian Doctrine*. Challenged historically by the collapse of Rome, he responded with the *City of God*. Ever since the First World War, secular prophets have warned of the collapse of our own civilization. Our challenge, like Augustine's, was not to recover a dying world but to mourn its loss, and simultaneously to affirm a faith that transcends every age.

Bibliographical Essay

Comprehensive Theologies

The comprehensive or systematic theology as a genre has been rarer than might be suspected. The following appear in chronological sequence. Each strongly suggests the relation of theology to secular thought.

Origen, *Peri Archon*.

Augustine, *On the Trinity*.

John of Damascus, *On the Orthodox Faith*.

Thomas Aquinas, *Summa Theologiae*.

John Calvin, *Institutes of the Christian Religion*.

Richard Hooker, *Laws of Ecclesiastical Polity*.

Joseph Butler, *Analogy of Religion*.

Karl Barth, *Dogmatics in Outline*.

Karl Rahner, *Foundations of the Christian Faith*.

Modern Theology

A useful guide to modern theological trends, sympathetic to interests represented in this work, is John Macquarrie's *Twentieth-Century Religious Thought*. Also useful is Aidan Nichol, *The Shape of Theology*, written from a Roman Catholic perspective.

Gustav Aulen, *Christus Victor*.

Anders Nygren, *Eros and Agape*.

Jurgen Moltmann, *Theology of Hope* and *The Crucified God*.

H. U. von Balthasar, *Herrlichkeit*.

Patristic Theology

There are several useful handbooks for patristics. A recommended history of the period is H. Chadwick's in the Pelican History of the Church series. Essential studies are G. Prestige, *God in Patristic Thought;* N. D. Kelly, *Early Christian Doctrines;* E. R. Dodd, *Pagan and Christian in an Age of Anxiety;* and C. N. Cochrane, *Christianity and Classical Culture.* W. H. Auden kept the latter on his nightstand as he wrote "For the Time Being."

Clement of Rome, *First Letter.*

Justin, *Apology.*

Irenaeus, *Against the Heresies.*

Origen, *On Prayer.*

Gregory of Nyssa, *Catechetical Oration.*

Basil the Great, sermons and commentaries.

Gregory the Great, *Moralia in Job* and *Pastoral Care.*

Augustine, *Confessions* and *On the Trinity.*

Medieval Theology

The close alignment of theology and philosophy in the Middle Ages means that studies in medieval philosophy, such as E. Gilson's *Spirit of Medieval Philosophy* and J. Pieper's *Scholasticism,* will shed much light on theology as well. Copleston's *Aquinas* is an excellent short introduction. Useful one-volume summaries of medieval thought are David Knowles, *Evolution of Medieval Thought;* and Gordon Leff, *Medieval Thought.*

St. Anselm, *Cur Deus Homo* and *Monologion.*

Peter Lombard, *Setences.*

Peter Abailard, *Ethics.*

Thomas Aquinas, *Summa contra Gentiles.*

Philosophy

The outstanding history of philosophy in English, Frederick Copleston's *History,* is sympathetic to medieval thought. A handy one-volume history of the early period, similarly sympathetic, is Armstrong's *Introduction to Ancient Philosophy.* A handy one-volume history of the entire field is D. W. Hamlyn's *History of Western Philosophy.*

Plato, the dialogues, especially *Meno, Phaedo, Timaeus.*

Aristotle, *Poetics; Logic; Nicomachean Ethics;* and *Metaphysics.*

Stoic thought is well-represented in the *Meditations* of Marcus Aurelius.

Epicurianism is expressed in poetic form in Lucretius's *De rerum natura.*

Modern philosophy begins with René Descartes, *Meditations* and *Discourse on Method.*

Other works of modern philosophy, mentioned in this work, which have interacted with theology include John Locke, *Essay Concerning Human Understanding* and *On the Reasonableness of Christianity;* George Berkeley, *Hylas and Philonus;* David Hume, *Treatise of Human Nature;* Immanuel Kant, *Critique of Pure Reason;* Arthur Schopenhauer, *World as Will and Idea;* and Friedrich Nietzsche, *Will to Power.*

Liturgical Study

The principle of *lex orandi* suggests the usefulness of a solid grounding in liturgical principles. The most helpful work for this purpose is M. Hatchett's *Sanctifying Time, Life, and Space,* a brilliantly syncretistic work. A comprehensive study is Jones, Wainwright, and Yarnold, *The Study of Liturgy.* A helpful essay is Evelyn Underhill, *Worship.* Hatchett's *Commentary on the American Prayer Book* is a mine of useful information, theologically sound throughout. Somewhat dated, but brought into useful perspective by Bishop Paul Marshall's editing and annotation, is Dom Gregory Dix, *The Shape of the Liturgy.*

Biblical Scholarship

A basic acquaintance with the theses and methods of modern scriptural study is essential for theology. A helpful introduction to the subject is Wright and Anderson's *Book of the Acts of God.* Almost as good is the volume on the Bible in the Church Teaching Series, *The Bible for Today's Church.* Old Testament theology is brilliantly presented in Gerhard von Rad's *Theology of the Old Testament*. R. Bultmann's *Theology of the New Testament* is now dated in its radicalism, but still interesting for its extreme assumptions. A monumental modern classic, W. F. Albright's *From the Stone Age to Christianity*, establishes, in minute detail, the archaeological contribution to theology. Karen Armstrong's *History of God*, finally, is a brilliant new contribution to scriptural theology, incorporating the results of scholarship into a comparative theological vision.